Collins

AF662407

Knowledge Lighthouse 4

A skill-based course on General Knowledge

Seema Chari
Kunal Savarkar

Student + Teacher

a animations

ilt instructor-led tutorials

ia activities

w worksheets

audio

g games

v videos

Teacher-only

lp lesson plans

w worksheets

tn teacher's notes

ak answer keys

Preface

There is no single route to knowledge and its sources are as diverse as the paths we adopt to gather and retain it, right from our family, school and friends to the Internet and books. General Knowledge is like common sense, but in times of multimedia, while it is easily available and accessible, it is not always easy to distinguish between real and fake, relevant and redundant, and interesting and inconsequential. We live in the digital age, which requires constant flexibility and adaptability.

Knowledge Lighthouse is a series meant for the Gen Z, or learners born in the new millennium. Their professional requirements are drastically different from those of earlier generations and require 'upskilling' throughout their lives. The series covers the general knowledge quotient of a spectrum of curricular as well as extra-curricular domains for learners of grades 1 to 8, with special emphasis on **21st century skills**. They are divided into three segments—learning skills, literacy skills and life skills. Through this series, we are certain that all learners can attain knowledge as the tasks are 'workoutable' and grade-appropriate.

General Knowledge provides context to school curriculum. ***Knowledge Lighthouse*** books are a repository of varied tasks divided in eight themes and skill pages. Our country is often presented in a complicated or insufficient way in GK books. This series showcases **India** content through colourful, simple and exciting tasks. Within the vast and varied India chapters are brand-new features such as **state-focus**, **city-focus** and **visit-a-monument**.

Science, technology, engineering and mathematics (**STEM**), the disciplines of the future that add a sprinkle of trivia to otherwise serious subjects have been covered extensively in grades 6-8.

The protection of our planet and sustainable development are critical issues that all of us need to think about and be aware of. **Save the Planet** theme aims to sensitise learners towards sustainable development throughout the series.

In the **Skills** pages, life skills has tasks on **safety** and **self-awareness**. Connecting the dots is the foundation of knowledge and the series has chapters based on **Higher Order Thinking Skills (HOTS)** and critical thinking to train young minds to see patterns, learn to eliminate or choose details and observe better.

Become a Champion Quizzer

Knowledge Lighthouse encourages all learners to be curious and explore the world around them. Those who observe and absorb all the time, learn from everyone and everything; they are the ones who become quizzers! Here are six rules that will help you become a champion quizzer.

1. Be curious—look around you, see everything, read everything.
2. Listen to others.
3. Seek out new experiences.
4. Learn to link events and people.
5. Do your own research and learn to spot fake news.
6. Remember, no matter how much you know, there is much more that you have yet to learn.

Now, go for it! We are sure that this series will expose a whole new generation of learners to the fun universe of general knowledge, and enhance their love for learning and discovery.

~ Kunal Savarkar and Seema Chari

In this series ...

Knowledge Lighthouse tasks are thematic and linear with visual, verbal, and strategic inputs to help students solve them and acquire knowledge through a wide range of subjects and themes.

World Around Us tasks take the learners on an exciting journey across the world.

Our Natural World section uncovers the magical realm of plants, animals and birds.

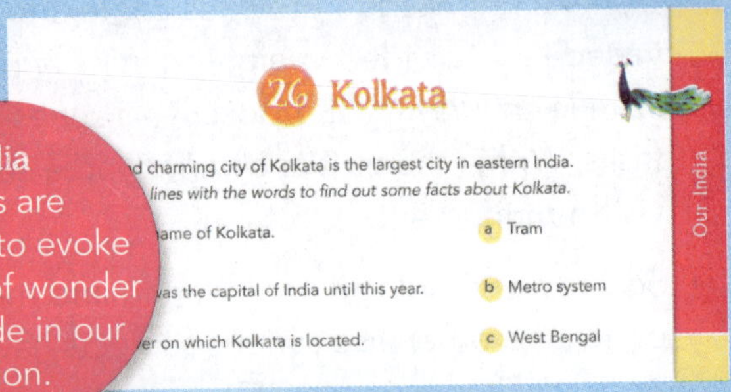

Save the Planet sensitises learners towards sustainable development of the planet.

India tasks are created to evoke a sense of wonder and pride in our nation.

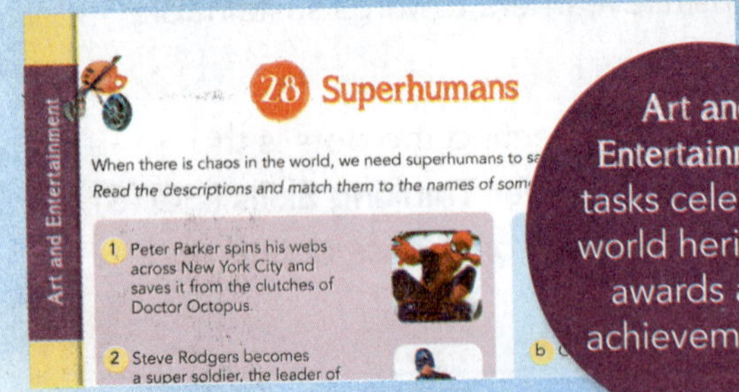

Art and Entertainment tasks celebrate world heritage, awards and achievements.

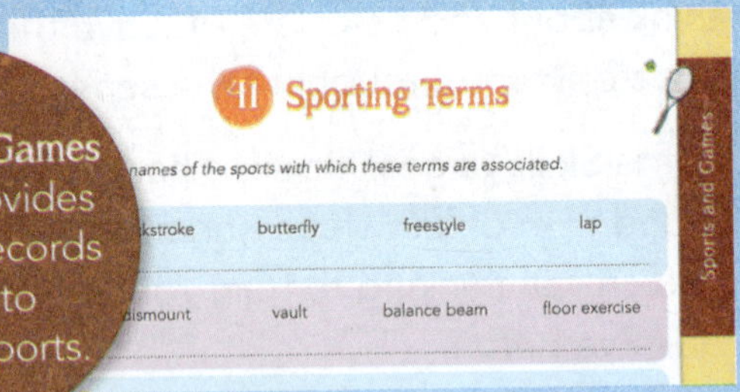

Sports and Games section provides rules and records related to different sports.

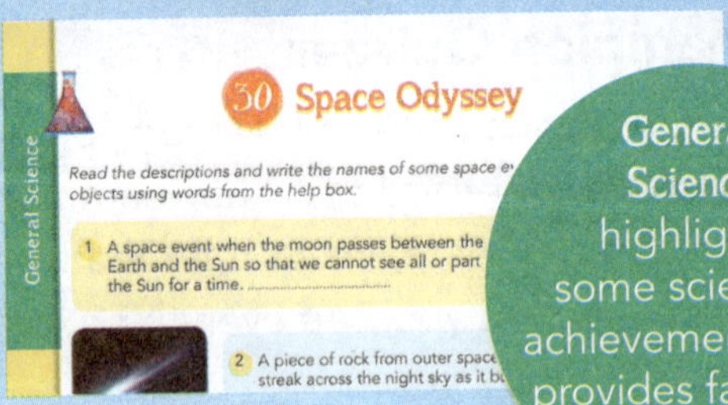

General Science highlights some scientific achievements and provides facts for others.

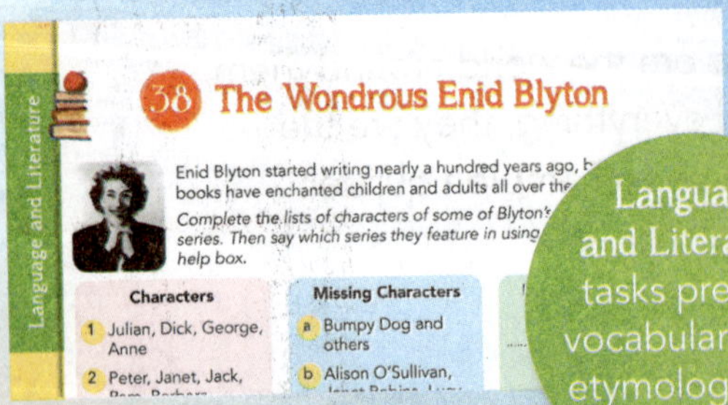

Language and Literature tasks present vocabulary and etymology in a fun way.

Whiz Fact is a spin-off fact about each topic or theme.

Whiz Quiz are fun activities that encourage self-learning.

21st Century Skills

21st century skills are necessary to succeed in the Age of Information. These skills are divided into three main sets, namely, learning skills, literacy skills and life skills.

Learning Skills

- Critical Thinking and HOTS
- Creativity
- Collaboration
- Communication

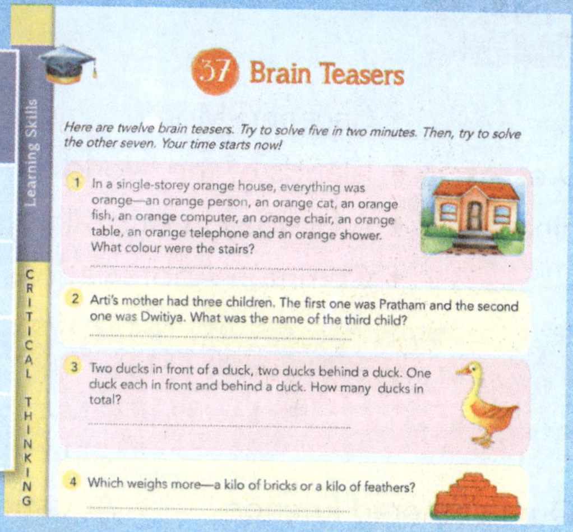

Learning Skills

CRITICAL THINKING

37 Brain Teasers

Here are twelve brain teasers. Try to solve five in two minutes. Then, try to solve the other seven. Your time starts now!

1. In a single-storey orange house, everything was orange—an orange person, an orange cat, an orange fish, an orange computer, an orange chair, an orange table, an orange telephone and an orange shower. What colour were the stairs?
2. Arti's mother had three children. The first one was Pratham and the second one was Dwitiya. What was the name of the third child?
3. Two ducks in front of a duck, two ducks behind a duck. One duck each in front and behind a duck. How many ducks in total?
4. Which weighs more—a kilo of bricks or a kilo of feathers?

Literacy Skills

- Technology
- Information
- Media

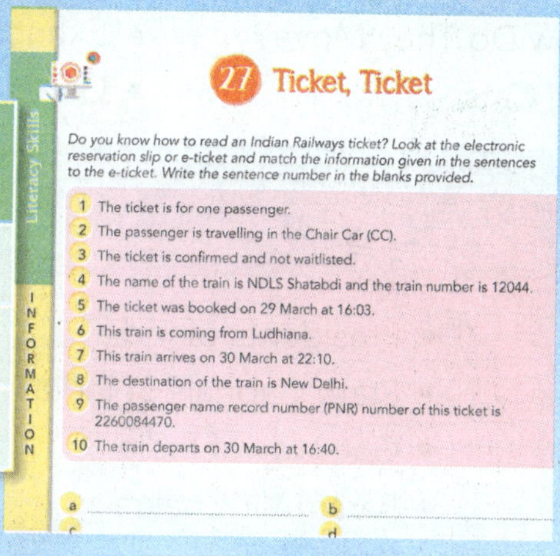

Literacy Skills

INFORMATION

27 Ticket, Ticket

Do you know how to read an Indian Railways ticket? Look at the electronic reservation slip or e-ticket and match the information given in the sentences to the e-ticket. Write the sentence number in the blanks provided.

1. The ticket is for one passenger.
2. The passenger is travelling in the Chair Car (CC).
3. The ticket is confirmed and not waitlisted.
4. The name of the train is NDLS Shatabdi and the train number is 12044.
5. The ticket was booked on 29 March at 16:03.
6. This train is coming from Ludhiana.
7. This train arrives on 30 March at 22:10.
8. The destination of the train is New Delhi.
9. The passenger name record number (PNR) number of this ticket is 2260084470.
10. The train departs on 30 March at 16:40.

a .... b ....

Life Skills

- Problem-solving
- Self-awareness
- Safety
- Social Skills

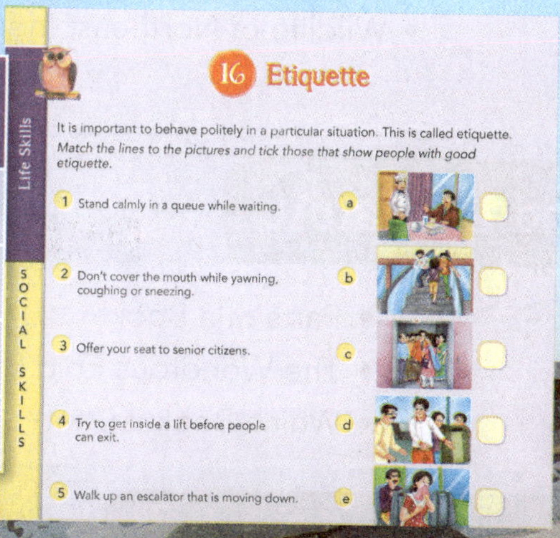

Life Skills

SOCIAL SKILLS

16 Etiquette

It is important to behave politely in a particular situation. This is called etiquette.
Match the lines to the pictures and tick those that show people with good etiquette.

1. Stand calmly in a queue while waiting. — a
2. Don't cover the mouth while yawning, coughing or sneezing. — b
3. Offer your seat to senior citizens. — c
4. Try to get inside a lift before people can exit. — d
5. Walk up an escalator that is moving down. — e

Detailed Contents

World Around Us

Our Natural World

Our India

Language and Literature

Art and Entertainment

Contents

1 Back and Forth

A palindrome is a word that reads the same backwards and forwards. Numbers, phrases and even sentences can be palindromes. Spaces and punctuation between the words is allowed. For example, the word 'refer' is a palindrome because it reads the same, whether you read it forwards or backwards.

Read the clues to find some palindromes and write them in the blanks provided.

1

A 3-letter-word that means 'mother'..

2

Another word for midday

....

3

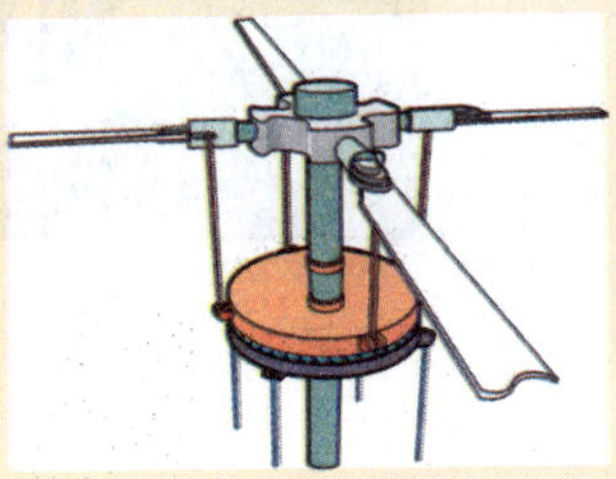

Four long blades which rotate and lift a helicopter off the ground ....

4

A narrow boat that moves with a double-bladed paddle

....

5

One of a series of stages in a game ....

6

A 3-letter-word used to express surprise ....

Whiz Fact

The longest palindrome is believed to be the Finnish word *saippuakivikauppias*, which means 'soapstone vendor'.

2 Our Feathered Friends

Read the clues and solve the rebus puzzles to find the names of these birds.

Clues	Rebus	Bird
1 A bird of prey with powerful talons and keen eyesight.		 = ...
2 A large water bird with a distinct pouch under its beak.	 – N + L I + 	 = ...
3 A long-legged bird that flies with its neck stretched.		 = ...
4 A medium-sized songbird.	 +  – M – E	 = ...

5 A nocturnal bird with a large flat and hooked beak, it gapes like the animal it is named after.

 + 

= ....

6 A bird with a long and thin neck which makes it look like a snake.

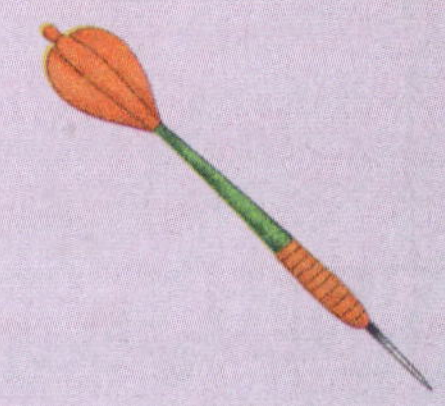 + ER

= ....

7 A kind of vulture, it is one of the largest flying land birds.

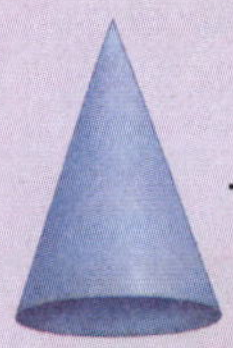 – E +  – O

= ....

8 The second-tallest living bird, it is Australia's largest native bird.

E +  – S I C

= ....

Whiz Fact

Weaver birds make interesting nests shaped like cans with a narrow entrance at the bottom. This makes it difficult for predators to enter the nest and eat their eggs or young ones.

3 Visiting the Doctor

Use the clues to complete the crossword about things we can see at a doctor's clinic.

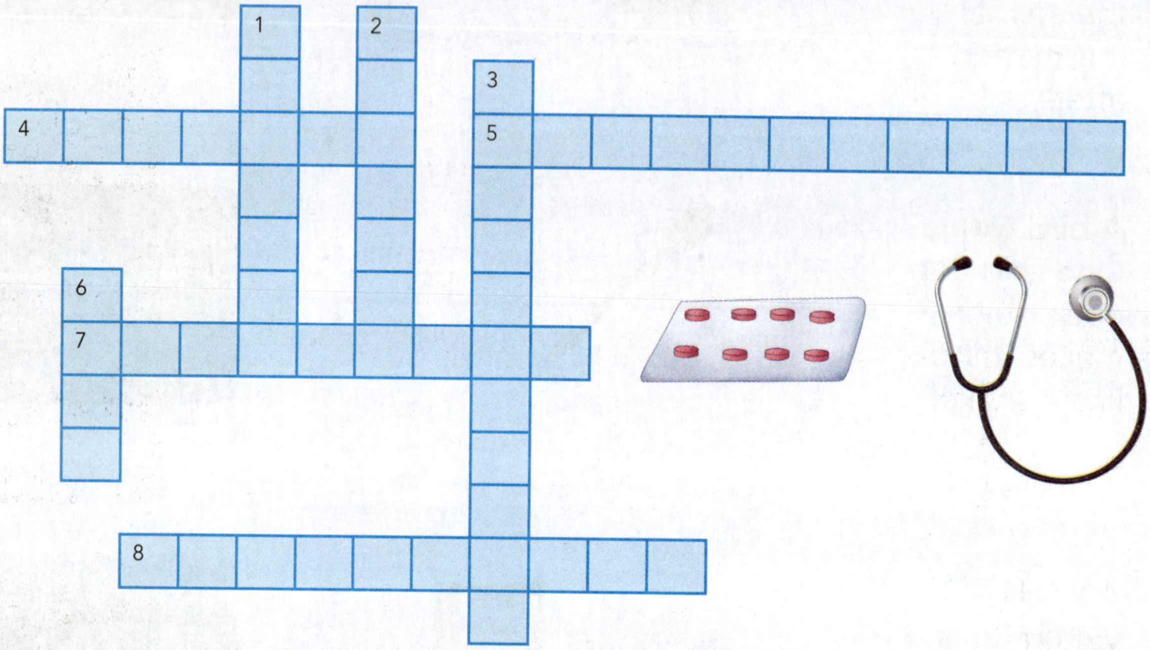

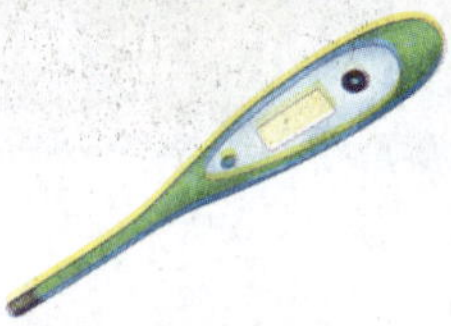

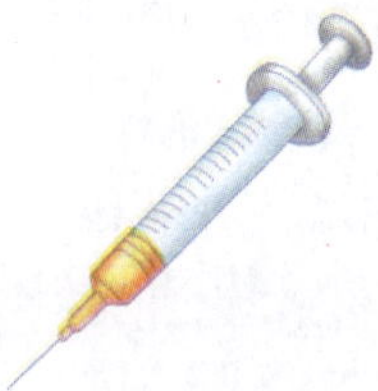

Across

4. A small tube with a thin hollow needle at the end
5. An instrument doctors use for measuring body temperature
7. When a doctor or a nurse puts medicine into our body using a device with a needle
8. A cream that helps to prevent infection in wounds

Down

1. A strip of cloth tied around a part of the body that has been hurt
2. A person who sells medicine
3. An instrument that a doctor uses to listen to somebody's heart and breathing
6. A small flat round piece of medicine that we swallow without chewing.

4 India in Colours

Many places in India have nicknames. Here are some of them. They are all names of colours.

Fill in the blanks using the words from the help box.

1. Jaipur is known as the .... Maharaja Jai Singh II had the city walls and buildings painted a light brick colour to welcome the Prince of Wales.

2. Jodhpur is known as the .... The houses in the old city are painted a bluish colour to keep them cool.

3. The Nilgiris are known as the .... The neelakurinji flower blooms every twelve years and gives the hilly slopes a brilliant blue-violet colour.

4. The town of Haldighati, where a famous battle was fought, was named for its .... soil. It looks like the colour of turmeric.

5. The .... runs from Kolkata to Dhanbad. Coal mines are found in this town.

6. The .... in Delhi is named after the red sandstone of which it is made.

Blue Mountains	Blue City	Black Diamond Express
Red Fort	yellow	Pink City

Whiz Fact

The English word orange is derived from the Sanskrit word *nãranga* which means an 'orange tree'.

5 How Do They Move?

Fill in the blanks with names of correct sea creatures.

Penguin

Jellyfish

Sea turtle

Octopus

1. A .... uses its fins to move through water, maintain balance and change direction.
2. A .... is a flightless bird that uses its flippers to swim in water.
3. A .... uses its short, stubby wing-like fins to swim in water.
4. An .... uses its webbed feet to jump on land and swim in water.
5. A .... is a sea creature with eight limbs that can walk on the ocean floor. Sometimes, it moves by sucking water and pushing it out.
6. A .... squeezes its body in order to push jets of water from the bottom of its body to move forward.
7. A .... thrusts its body from side to side in an S-shaped movement to push itself forward.
8. A .... moves its whole body in a wave-like motion to move through water.

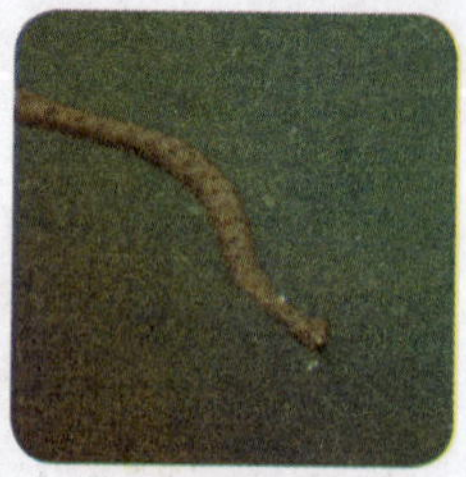
Snake

Fish

Stingray

Frog

Whiz Fact

The Portuguese man o' war is a jellyfish-like creature which does not really swim. It has a bladder which inflates and deflates depending on whether it wants to be closer to or farther away from the sea's surface.

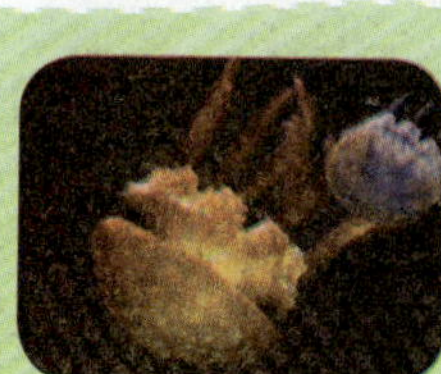

6 Gender Nouns

It's been raining for 40 days and the animal pairs need to board Noah's Ark lest they drown.

Read the names of animals and write their gender names with the help of the clues and words from the help box.

Animals	Female	Male
1 Donkey	a	i Jack
2 Bear	b Sow	ii ....
3 Chicken	c	iii ....
4 Camel	d	iv Bull
5 Deer	e Doe	v ....
6 Fox	f	vi ....
7 Goose	g	vii ....
8 Goat	h Nanny	viii ....
9 Horse	i Mare	ix ....
10 Sheep	j	x ....
11 Swan	k	xi Cob
12 Bee	l	xii Drone

Stallion Vixen Cow Jenny Queen Buck Ewe Rooster
Goose Billy Dog Pen Ram Hen Boar Gander

Whiz Fact

In ant and bee colonies, only one female is the queen and others are called workers or drones. This is the origin of the phrase 'to be the queen bee', meaning to get others to do as you wish.

7 Big Cats

There are many species of cats, but some are called big cats. All big cats are carnivores. They are found in North America, South America, Africa, and Asia.

Read the clues and write the names of some big cats in the crossword puzzle. The first letter of each answer has been given for you.

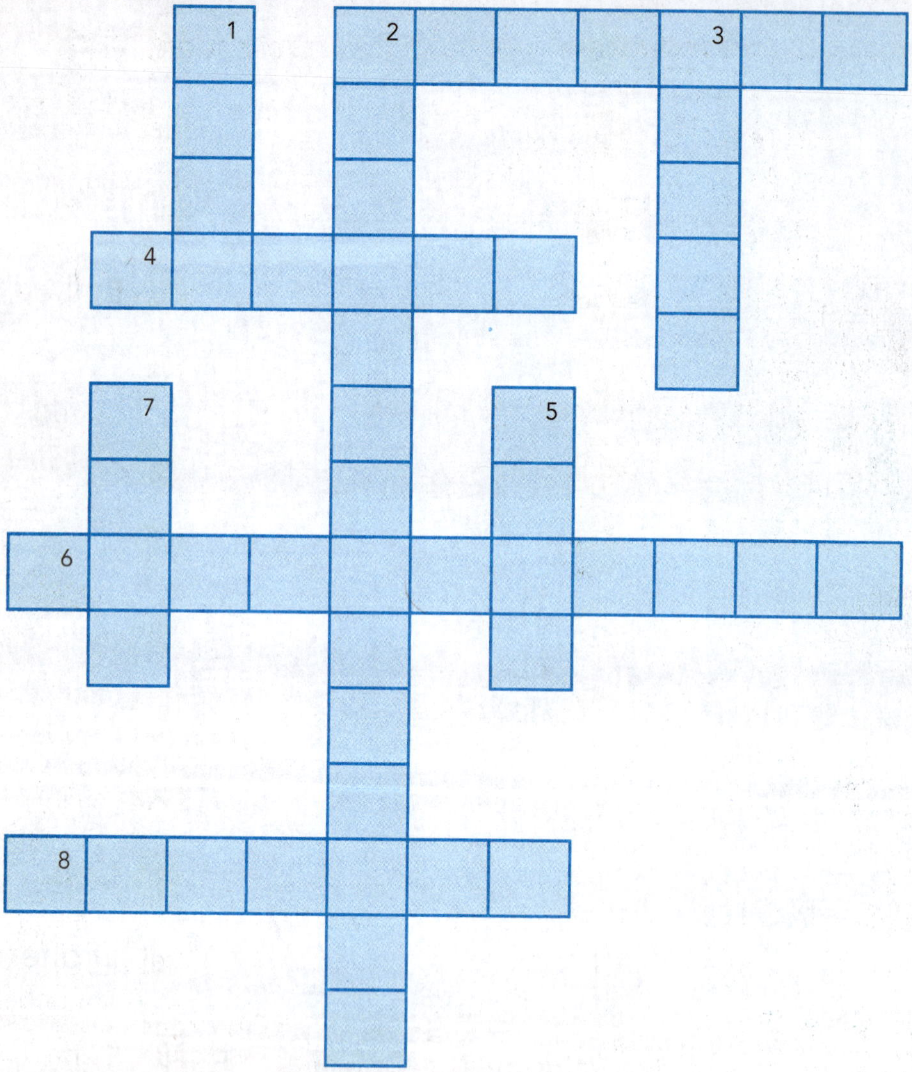

Whiz Fact

The cat family is also called the feline family. Most members of this family are patterned with spots, stripes or rosettes on their body. The rusty-spotted cat is its smallest member.

Across

2 The fastest land animal, it runs at a speed of nearly 113 km per hour.

4 The national animal of Guyana, it has yellowish-brown fur with black rings and spots.

6 A big cat that lives in the cold deserts of Asia, it is often called 'ghost of the mountain' because it is rarely seen.

8 A big cat with dark spots called rosettes, which create a beautiful pattern against its light fur.

Down

1 A big cat that is also known as mountain lion or cougar. It has brownish-grey fur.

2 A big cat which is more at home on trees than on the ground, it has the longest canine teeth of any living feline.

3 The largest member of the cat family known by its stripes.

5 It is the only big cat with a mane.

7 A big cat with a short tail and large pointy ears.

8 World Traditional Dresses

We can wear clothes made in different places today, thanks to trade and travel. In many communities around the world, there are clothes for special occasions or simply for a change in weather conditions.

Match the pictures to the descriptions and identify the countries in which these clothes are worn using their flags as clues.

Traditional Dresses	Descriptions	Flags
1 	a The elegant *traje de flamenca* is a long dress with ruffles worn by women in Andalusia.	i  Japan
2 	b The kimono is a wraparound dress worn with a sash.	ii  Scotland
3 	c The kilt is a kind of skirt worn by men.	iii  Bhutan
4 	d The *gho* is a dress worn by men in a country in the Himalayan region.	iv  Spain

5 

e The *sarafan* is a long dress worn by women in a transcontinental country located In Europe and Asia.

v 

Mexico

6 

f The sari is a single length of fabric that can be draped in dozens of different ways.

vi 

Russia

7 

g The *huipil* is a colourful embroidered loose-fitting tunic worn by indigenous women of Central America.

vii 

South Korea

8 

h The *hanbok* is an outfit consisting of a fitted blouse and a flared skirt.

viii 

India

Whiz Quiz

In which of these countries in southeast Asia is a conical hat called *non la* worn?

a Malaysia b Indonesia c Vietnam

Whiz Fact

The kanga is a colourful outfit worn in different countries around the African Great Lakes. The earliest patterns made on the kanga resembled the speckled plumage of a bird called Guinea fowl.

9 Using Money

Seema carries the same amount of money in her wallet everyday. Read the purchases she made and write the values of notes and coins she used for payments. On every purchase, Seema paid exact change.

Seema's Wallet

Purchases

2 January

1 Seema bought a bouquet of flowers for ₹220.

Notes ....

Coins ....

14 January

2 Seema bought a birthday gift for ₹572.

Notes ....

Coins ....

22 January

3. Seema visited a dentist's clinic. She paid ₹800 as the dentist's fee.

Notes ....

Coins ....

5 February

4. Seema bought a bedcover for ₹2,500 for her parents.

Notes ....

Coins ....

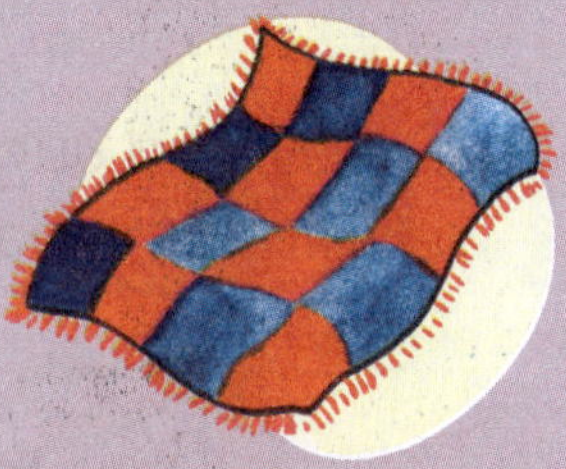

16 February

5. Seema bought a box of pencils for ₹22.

Notes ....

Coins ....

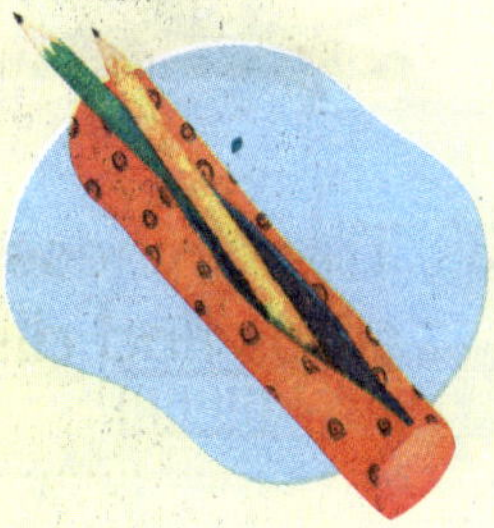

20 March

6. Seema went to a restaurant for dinner and paid a bill of ₹2,110.

Notes ....

Coins ....

Whiz Quiz

Which new banknote issued by the Reserve Bank of India does not have a picture of a monument on the reverse side?

10 Our Neighbour, China

China is India's largest neighbour. It is also one of the few countries that is larger than India, and the only country to have a larger population than India.

Fill in the blanks with the help of the clues and the words from help box to know more about China.

1 Crispy and sugary, they are served after a Chinese meal.

....

2 A powerful creature from the Chinese mythology often linked to the Emperor

....

3 The Chinese invented this device that helped ships find directions.

....

4 A traditional Chinese dress

....

5 The Chinese emperor Shennong discovered it after he saw a leaf falling in boiling water.

....

6 The Chinese invented this huge aircraft that carries passengers in a basket.

....

7 The Chinese eat with this pair of thin sticks.

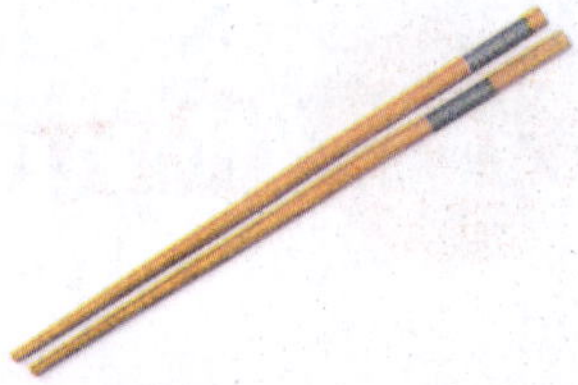

8 A festival that marks the end of the Chinese New Year.

9 The most important bird in Chinese legend.

10 Regarded a Wonder of the World, its length spans several thousand kilometres.

11 A high-ranking official in the former imperial Chinese government; shares its name with China's official language.

12 In ancient China, this flower was considered a symbol of purity.

Mandarin	Dragon	Chopsticks	Lotus	Tea
Lantern Festival	Fortune Cookie	Hot-Air Balloon		
Chinese Phoenix	Cheongsam	Compass	Great Wall of China	

Whiz Fact

Red is considered a lucky colour in Chinese culture. It is used widely during festivals like the Lantern Festival, the Chinese New Year and even in weddings.

11 Enjoy the Festivities

India is a land of many festivals. Here are names of some common and some lesser-known festivals.

Read the clues and write the names of the festivals using words from the help box.

1 A festival celebrating the bond between brothers and sisters.

....

2 A festival marking the new year in Kerala celebrated in April.

....

3 A festival marking the end of the holy month of Ramzan.

....

4 The birth of Zoroaster, founder of the Parsi religion called Zoroastrianism

....

5 An Odia festival commemorating the annual visit of Lord Jagannath of Puri to the Gundicha Temple in Puri. The deity is accompanied by his sister and elder brother—all on their chariots.

....

6 The birth of Krishna celebrated by re-enacting scenes from his birth and singing devotional songs in temples.

....

Whiz Fact

Makar Sankranti is also called Thai Pongal in Tamil Nadu and Magh Bihu in Assam.

7 The birth of Guru Nanak, the first Sikh Guru and the founder of Sikhism.

....

8 The beginning of the Telugu and Kannada new years, the festival is called Gudi Padwa in Maharashtra.

....

9 A festival celebrating the birthday of the founder of Jainism.

....

10 The birth of Prophet Muhammad, the founder of Islam.

....

11 The birth of Jesus Christ born in Bethlehem.

....

12 A festival marking the harvest season and the end of winter in Punjab.

....

13 Shivaratri, as celebrated by the people of Jammu and Kashmir.

....

Eid-ul-Fitr Khordad Sal Rath Yatra Janamashtami
Bhai Dooj Gurpurab Herath Ugadi Mahavir Jayanti
Vishu Milad-un-Nabi Lohri Christmas

12 Name Mnemonics

A mnemonic helps us remember information easily. There are many types of mnemonics.

Read these mnemonics and find out what they stand for using words from the help box.

1 My Very Excited Mother Just Served Us Noodles

The eight .... of the solar system are Mercury, Venus, Earth, Mars, Jupiter, Saturn, Uranus and Neptune.

2 Super Man Helps Every One

The .... of North America from west to east are Superior, Michigan, Huron, Erie and Ontario.

3 Lazy Cats Do not Move

The .... in multiples of 10 are L = 50, C = 100, D = 500 and M = 1000.

4 Big Gorillas Eat Hotdogs Not Cold Pizza

The seven countries of .... are Belize, Guatemala, El Salvador, Honduras, Nicaragua, Costa Rica and Panama

5 Prime Ministers Cannot Eat Any Nachos

The time zones of .... from west to east are Pacific, Mountain, Central, Eastern, Atlantic and Newfoundland.

6 No Soup For Russia

Northern .... countries from west to east are Norway, Sweden, Finland and Russia.

7 Incredibly Slimy Cockroach Bit My Aunt

The countries around the .... are Italy, Slovenia, Bosnia and Herzegovina, Montenegro and Albania.

Great Lakes   Canada   planets   Central America   Roman numerals   European   Adriatic Sea

Whiz Quiz

Make a mnemonic for the union territories of India.

....

....

....

....

Whiz Fact

A mnemonic for remembering the steps for treating a sprain is the word 'rice'.

Rest the sprained part

Ice the sprained area

Compress with a bandage

Elevate the sprained part

13 Aquatic Water Plants

Aquatic plants are plants that grow in saltwater or freshwater. Submerged plants grow fully under water. Emergent plants are rooted in the soil below the water body, but their leaves and stems extend out of the water.

Match these aquatic floral plants to their descriptions.

1 

Water poppy

2 

Buttonbush

3 

Watercress

4 

Cardinal flower

5 

Water hyacinth

a A common North American shrub having dense, round clusters of small hairy white flowers.

b A floating aquatic plant with swollen leafstalks, it forms dense masses in rivers and ponds.

c This plant grows in the wetlands, its bright-red flowers grow at the end of long stems.

d This plant has lemon-yellow coloured flowers with red-brown centres and dark green, round leaves.

e A small plant with white flowers which grows in streams and pools. Its leaves taste hot and are eaten raw in salads.

6 

Lizard's tail

7 

Japanese iris

8 

Pickerelweed

9 

Water hawthorn

10 

Water lily

f A North American freshwater plant having arrow-shaped leaves and purple flowers. It shares its name with a fish.

g An ornamental plant with large flat leaves and colourful cup-shaped flowers which floats on the surface of lakes and rivers.

h This plant has long shiny leaves and produces tiny, tube-like Y-shaped blue flowers on spikes.

i This plant has dark green leaves and showy clusters of blue or purple, broad trumpet-shaped flowers.

j The flowers of this plant grow in a bottle-brush spike of white flowers. The flower spike arches above the leaves of the plant.

Whiz Quiz Find out why most aquatic plants have spongy leaves and stems.

Whiz Fact Submerged plants, especially those that grow in deep oceans, do not get much sunlight, yet they undergo photosynthesis.

14 Road Signs

Road signs keep the roads safe for pedestrians and drivers. They are of three types—circular signs, triangular signs and rectangular signs.

Circular signs

Circular signs are compulsory signs. They show information everyone must follow.

Triangular signs

Triangular signs are cautionary signs. They warn people about unsafe conditions on the road.

Rectangular signs

Rectangular signs are informatory signs. They show information regarding nearby places. They also show driving directions to places in the city or nearby cities.

Whiz Fact

The stop sign is the only eight-sided sign. It asks drivers to stop.

Look at the signs and write what they mean using words from help box. Be careful of extra words in the help box.

1 

....

2 

....

3 

....

4 

....

5 

....

6 

....

7 

....

8 

....

9 

....

Speed breaker ahead   Pedestrian crossing prohibited   No right turn
Payment counter   Zebra crossing   Parking   Cows can rest here
Animal crossing   No U-turn   Narrow road ahead
No left turn   Airport ahead

Whiz Fact

A 'give way' sign indicates that vehicles should slow down or stop in order to allow other vehicles to pass in front of them. A 'give way' sign looks like an upside down triangle.

15 Great Lines

The leaders of India said some great lines or slogans that are still famous.

Complete each slogan using words from the help box. The meanings and names of the leader who gave each slogan are given.

	Slogans	Meanings	Who Said It?
1	*Jai*	Victory to India!	 Subhas Chandra Bose
2	*Satyameva*	Truth alone triumphs.	 Madan Mohan Malviya

Whiz Fact

The national motto of India, *Satyameva Jayate*, which translates to 'Truth alone triumphs', is a very old saying. It is inscribed on the base of India's national emblem. One can read it in Sanskrit on all banknotes of India.

3

Inquilab ....

Long live the revolution!

Bhagat Singh

4

Vande ....

Hail my motherland!

Bankim Chandra Chattopadhyay

5

Jai Jawaan Jai ....

Victory to the soldier,

Victory to the farmer!

Lal Bahadur Shastri

Kisaan *Zindabad* *Hind* *Mataram* *Jayate*

16 Etiquette

It is important to behave politely in a particular situation. This is called etiquette.

Match the lines to the pictures and tick those that show people with good etiquette.

1. Stand calmly in a queue while waiting.
2. Don't cover your mouth while yawning, coughing or sneezing.
3. Offer your seat to senior citizens.
4. Try to get inside a lift before people can exit.
5. Walk up an escalator that is moving down.
6. Scold the waiter if you do not like your food.

a  ☐

b  ☐

c  ☐

d  ☐

e  ☐

f  ☐

Whiz Fact

The word 'etiquette' is derived from French, in which it means 'tag' or 'label'. Etiquette has no plural form.

17 Singing for India

Some songs make us feel proud as Indians.

Read the lines about some of these songs and fill in the blanks using words from the help box.

1. The national anthem of India, *Jana gana mana* was written in .... and composed by ....

2. The national anthem was first sung publicly in 1911. The full version of the anthem takes .... seconds to be performed.

3. The poet .... composed the song *Sare Jahan se Achha* in ....in the year 1904.

4. The tune of *Sare Jahan se Achha* was composed by the great musician .... The song is also called .... , which means an 'Anthem of Indians'.

5. The writer and poet .... wrote *Vande Mataram* in an 1881 novel called ....

6. *Vande Mataram* was adopted as the national song in ....

Anandamath   *Taranah-e-Hindi*   Ravi Shankar   52   Urdu
Rabindranath Tagore   Bengali   Bankim Chandra Chattopadhyay
Muhammad Iqbal   1937

Whiz Fact

The National Anthem of Bangladesh is called *Amar Shonar Bangla*. It was composed by Rabindranath Tagore.

18 Cars and More

Match the descriptions of the car logos to the names of their manufacturing companies.

1 Fiat	a A slanting H
2 Toyota	b A stylised S
3 Suzuki	c The four letters of its name
4 Honda	d One letter inside another
5 Volkswagen	e Two ovals that make up a T
6 Hyundai	f A plump and squat H

7 Audi

8 Volvo

9 Renault

10 Ferrari

11 Jaguar

12 Chevrolet

13 Ford

g Plus sign

h Four rings

i Name written in running hand

j Name written in print

k A diamond

l An animal's face or a leaping animal

m A prancing horse

Whiz Fact

Henry Ford was the first person to manufacture automobiles on a mass scale in a factory. This was called an assembly line.

19 Once Upon a Time

Read the opening lines of some famous books and write the names of the books. Be careful because there are more books than the opening lines. Choose your books from the bookshelf.

1 "Where's Papa going with that ax?" said Fern to her mother as they were setting the table for breakfast.

....

2 In an old house in Paris that was covered with vines lived twelve little girls in two straight lines.

....

3 All children, except one, grow up.

....

4 First of all, let me get something straight: this is a JOURNAL, not a diary.

....

5 Dorothy lived in the midst of the great Kansas prairies, with Uncle Henry, who was a farmer, and Aunt Em, who was the farmer's wife.

....

6 It's a funny thing about mothers and fathers.

....

7 The sun did not shine.
It was too wet to play.
So we sat in the house
All that cold, cold wet day.

....

8 Mr. and Mrs. Dursley, of number four, Privet Drive, were proud to say that they were perfectly normal, thank you very much.

....

9 Look, I didn't want to be a half-blood.

....

10 Now Chil the Kite brings home the night That Man the Bat sets free –
The herds are shut in byre and hut, For loosed till dawn are we.

....

Whiz Quiz

"Macavity's a Mystery Cat: he's called the Hidden Paw", are the opening lines of the popular poem 'Macavity'. Who wrote the poem?

a William Wordsworth b Daphne du Maurier c T.S. Eliot

Whiz Fact

The first sentence of L.M. Montgomery's *Anne of the Green Gables* has 148 words!

20 Northward Ho!

North India is known for its crafts and many wonderful places.

Read the descriptions and write the names of regions to which these tourist destinations and crafts belong using names from the help box.

Tourist Destinations

1

The Golden Temple is in Amritsar, close to the India-Pakistan border.

....

3

Naini Lake is in the Kumaon region, in the lap of the Himalayas.

....

5

Fatehpur Sikri is close to Agra.

....

Crafts

2

Garhwal paintings are made in the Garhwal Himalayas, near India's border with Nepal.

....

4

Gold and silver embroidery on silk is a speciality of sarees from Banaras and nearby towns.

....

6

Papier mâché is a special craft of India's northernmost union territory.

....

7

The monasteries of Dharamshala are in the Kangra district. Dharamshala's most famous resident is the Dalai Lama.

....

8

Woollen shawls with colourful motifs are specially woven in the Kullu Valley.

....

9

Zanskar Valley is close to Tibet.

....

10

Phulkari embroidery is popular in cities like Patiala, Jalandhar, Nabha and Ludhiana.

....

Jammu and Kashmir   Himachal Pradesh
Punjab   Uttarakhand   Uttar Pradesh   Ladakh

Whiz Quiz Which state in north India is known as the 'land of five rivers'?

Whiz Fact Houseboats made of wood are moored along the shore of the Dal Lake in Srinagar, Jammu and Kashmir. These are homes of different sizes, with bedrooms, bathrooms, a living room and a kitchen.

21 Islands of the World

An island is a piece of land surrounded by water. Islands are mostly found in seas and oceans, but they can also be found in rivers and lakes.

Read the lines and write the names of these islands using words from the help box.

1 Two islands of Indonesia

.... and ....

2 Japan's biggest island

....

3 An island in the Caribbean Sea

....

4 A large island in the Indian Ocean

....

5 An island in the Atlantic Ocean, west of Great Britain

....

6 An island immediately south of India

....

7 An island in the Mediterranean Sea

....

8 An island to the east of mainland China

....

Taiwan Sri Lanka Madagascar Borneo Honshu
Ireland Sumatra Cyprus Jamaica

Whiz Fact

Treasure Island, *Robinson Crusoe* and *The Swiss Family Robinson* are novels in which most of the story takes place on an island.

22 Appsolutely Great

Mobile phones and smartphones have many apps.

Read the clues and write the names of apps using words from the help box.

1 This app has a fat white letter F on a blue box.

....

2 This chat-app has a green and white logo with a phone receiver in a chat box.

....

3 This browser app has a circle with red, green and yellow parts and a small blue circle at the centre.

....

4 This app has a little bird with a pointy beak.

....

5 This app helps us find a place. It has a green, red and grey map with a pin and the letter G on it.

....

6 This video app has a red box with a white play symbol in it.

....

YouTube Google Chrome WhatsApp
Facebook Twitter Google Maps

23 Extinct Animals

These animals that once roamed the Earth in large numbers are extinct because of destruction of their habitat and hunting.

Read the descriptions and write the names of these extinct animals.

1 A striking animal, it was a half-zebra and half-horse and got its name from the sound it made.

.... A G G A

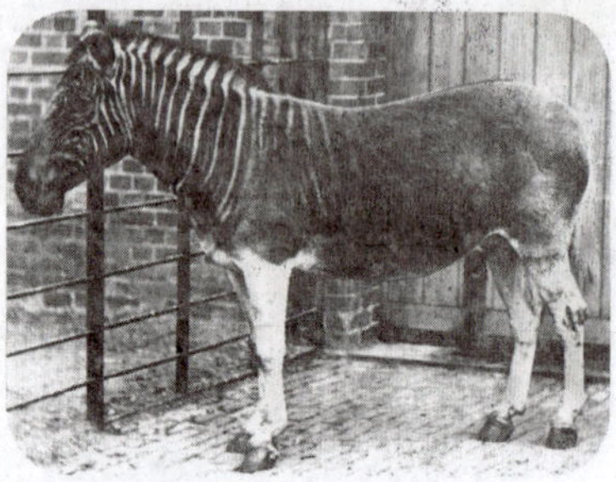

2 This huge species of flightless bird native to New Zealand grew taller than the elephants of today.

.... O A

3 Despite its name, it looked more like a bear with short powerful limbs.

SA .... RE-TOOT .... ED CAT

4 This animal was one of the heaviest and largest animals of its type in the country where it lived; it had silvery fur.

ME .... CAN GRI .... ZLY BEAR

5 The last known bird of this species died in the wild around 1900 and by 1914 the last captive bird died.

PA .... SENGER .... IGEO ....

6 This huge, plant-eating sea mammal was hunted to extinction within three decades of its discovery.

STE .... LER 'S SEA- .... OW

7 This big cat lived on the Sunda Islands of Indonesia.

JA .... AN TIGER

8 This flightless bird resembled the penguin, but it had a heavy hooked beak.

.... REAT AUK

9 This flightless bird inhabited Mauritius.

DO .... O

10 This elephant-like creature had long tusks and was covered in black, brown and ginger fur.

.... OOLL .... M .... MM .... TH

11 This giant deer could grow to a height of 7 ft and weigh up to 700 kgs.

I .... ISH EL ....

12 This animal has shrines dedicated to it because it is regarded as a messenger of the spirits.

.... APAN .... SE HONSHU WOL ....

Whiz Fact

The Pyrenean ibex is the only species ever to become 'un-extinct' after being cloned in 2009. Unfortunately, the clone lived only for seven minutes and the species became extinct once again.

24 Mountains of India

Mountains are tall and steep chunks of land. Groups of mountains are called chains or ranges. India has many mountain ranges.

Look at the map, read the clues and write the names of the mountain ranges.

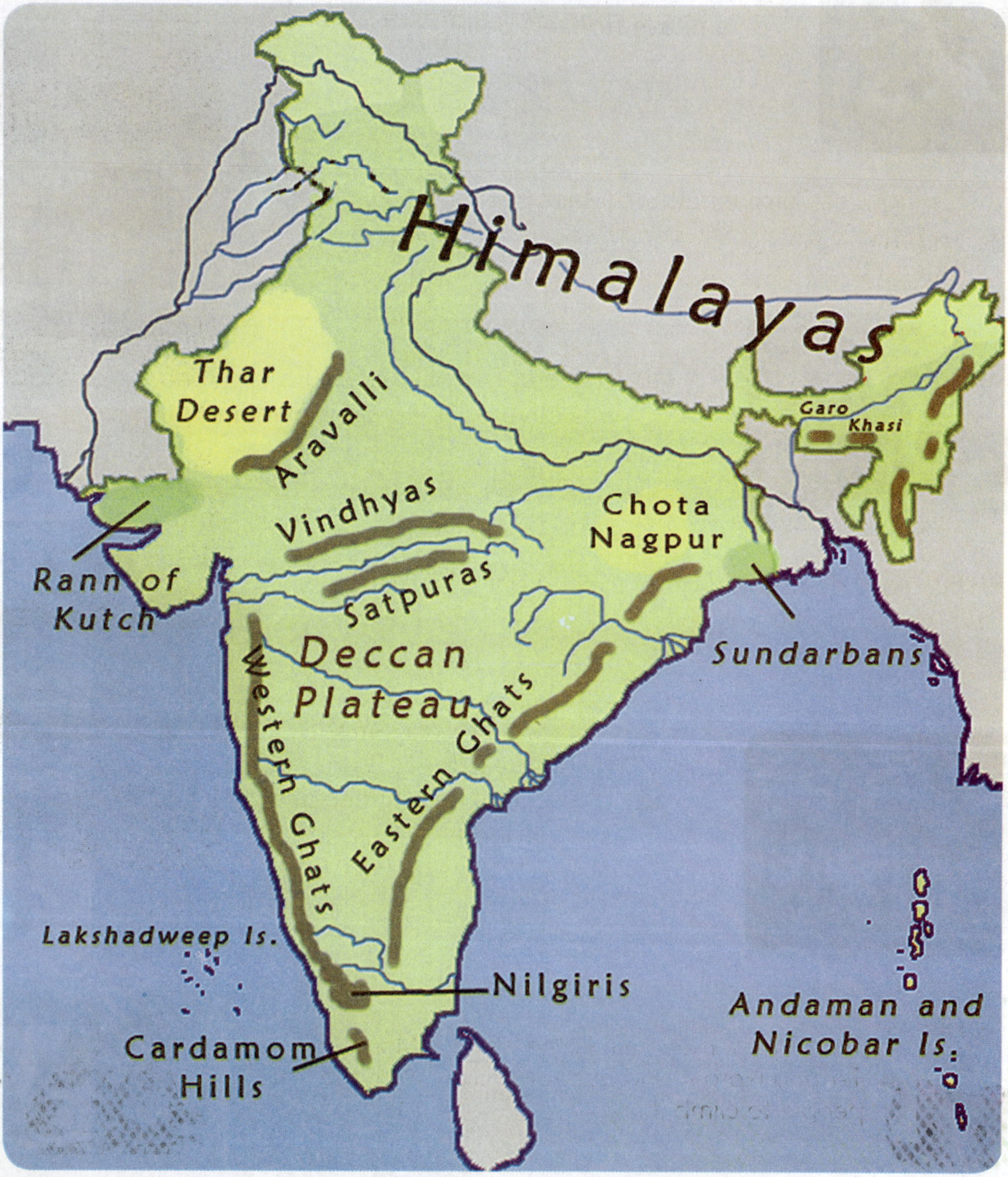

1 The chain of the tallest mountains in the world, its name means 'Land of Snow'.

....

2 The two mountain ranges stretching along the eastern and western coasts of India.

....

3 The mountain range that divides India into two parts—north and south. The name of this mountain range is mentioned in the national anthem of India.

....

4 The mountain ranges located in the northeast of India.

....

5 This range has some of the oldest mountains in the world. It stretches across Gujarat, Rajasthan, Delhi and Haryana.

....

Whiz Fact

The highest mountain in the world is Mount Everest. Tenzing Norgay and Edmund Hillary were the first people to climb it.

25 Parts of a Book

Use the clues and words from the help box to solve the crossword and find out the names of different parts of a book.

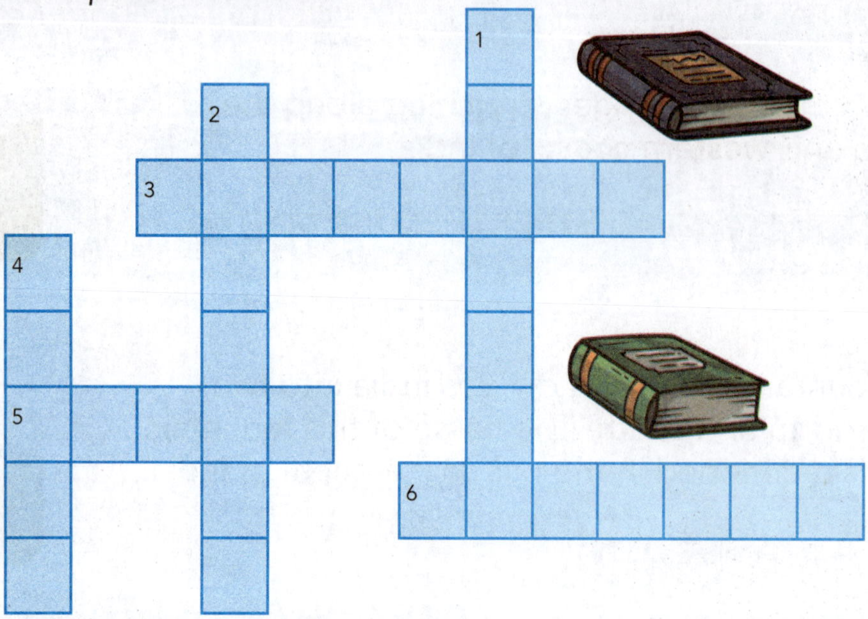

Across

3 A list of special words and their meanings.

5 An alphabetical list printed at the back of a book which indicates the pages on which important topics are referred to.

6 An introduction to the book that describes it in brief and explains the reason for which it was written.

Down

1 Parts into which a book is divided.

2 A blank page at the beginning and the end of the book.

4 The backbone of the book where its title is visible when it is upright.

spine | preface | index | glossary | chapter | flyleaf

Whiz Fact

A prologue is a speech or a section of text that introduces a book. An epilogue is a passage or speech which is added to the end of a book as a conclusion.

26 Kolkata

The old and charming city of Kolkata is the largest city in eastern India.

Match these lines with the words to find out some facts about Kolkata.

1	The old name of Kolkata	a	Tram
2	Kolkata was the capital of India until this year.	b	Metro system
3	The river on which Kolkata is located	c	West Bengal
4	A famous bridge in Kolkata	d	City of Joy
5	A type of that train only Kolkata has	e	Howrah
6	Kolkata was India's first city to have this public transport system.	f	Calcutta
7	Kolkata is the capital of this state.	g	Hooghly
8	A sobriquet of Kolkata	h	1911

Whiz Fact

Eden Gardens is India's first and second largest, and the world's third largest cricket stadium after the Sardar Patel Stadium in Ahmedabad and the Melbourne Cricket Ground.

27 Ticket, Ticket

Do you know how to read an Indian Railways ticket? Look at the components of the electronic reservation slip or e-ticket and match the information given in the sentences to the e-ticket. Write the sentence number in the boxes provided.

1. The ticket is for one passenger.
2. The passenger is travelling in the Chair Car (CC).
3. The ticket is confirmed and not waitlisted.
4. The name of the train is NDLS Shatabdi and the train number is 12044.
5. The ticket was booked on 29 March at 16:03.
6. This train is coming from Ludhiana.
7. This train arrives on 30 March at 22:10.
8. The destination of the train is New Delhi.
9. The passenger name record number (PNR) number of this ticket is 2260084470.
10. The train departs on 30 March at 16:40.

a ☐ b ☐ c ☐

d ☐ e ☐ f ☐

g ☐ h ☐ i ☐

j ☐

Whiz Fact

As of February 2019, the fastest train in India is the Vande Bharat Express that runs between Delhi and Varanasi.

Electronic Reservation Slip IRCTC

30 **PNR No.** 2260084470 (a)	(b) **Train No. & Name:** 12044/ NDLS SHATABDI	**Quota:** GENERAL (GN)
Transaction ID: XXXXX	**Date & Time of Booking:** (c) 29-Mar-2019 16:03	**Class of Travel:** (d) CHAIR CAR (CC)
From: (e) LUDHIANA JN	**Date of Journey:** 30-Mar-2019	**To:** NEW DELHI (f)
Adult: 1 **Child:** 0 (g)	**Scheduled Arrival:** 30-Mar-2019 22:10 (h)	**Scheduled Departure:** 30-Mar-2019 16:40 (i)

Passenger Details

S. No.	Name	Age	Sex	Booking Status	Current Status
1	Ramesh Das	31	MALE	CNF/C9/36/ Window Side	CNF/C9/36/Window Side (j)

Whiz Quiz Find out the name of the mascot of the Indian Railways.

28 Superhumans

When there is chaos in the world, we need superhumans to save the planet.

Read the descriptions and match them to the names of some superhumans.

1 Peter Parker spins his webs across New York City and saves it from the clutches of Doctor Octopus.

2 Steve Rodgers becomes a super soldier, the leader of the Avengers.

3 Tony Stark is a genius and billionaire who along with his virtual assistant, Edwin Jarvis, always saves the day.

4 Half-human and half-alien, Carol Danvers is one of the most powerful members of the Avengers. Thanks to her, the mighty Thanos was defeated.

5 The son of Odin and god of thunder, his hammer Mjolnir helps him win against his enemies.

a Iron Man

b Captain Marvel

c Thor

d Captain America

e Spider-Man

Whiz Fact

The Incredibles is a film series about super-beings who have been ordered not to use their superpowers, but are finally forced to use them. Well, save the world.

6 Billionaire Bruce Wayne becomes the Dark Knight to protect Gotham from the Joker.

7 Kal-El was born on the planet Krypton. He comes to Earth and becomes the Man of Steel.

8 Princess Diana uses her Lasso of Truth to tie up her enemies. She is the leader of the Amazons.

9 Barry Allen is the fastest man alive and uses his super speed to save Central City.

10 Arthur Curry is the King of the underwater kingdom Atlantis. He uses the Trident of Neptune to protect all the creatures of the sea.

11 Dr. Robert Bruce Banner transforms into a huge, green-skinned humanoid possessing great strength.

f Aquaman

g Flash Gordon

h Batman

i Incredible Hulk

j Wonder Woman

k Superman

Whiz Quiz

These superhumans are from two 'universes'—the Marvel Universe and the DC Universe. Can you say which characters are from which universe?

29 A Holiday in Australia

Read the clues and look at the map to find out some facts about Australia.

1 The city on the westernmost coast of Australia.

.... E R ....

2 An island in the Southern Ocean which is a part of Australia.

.... A S .... N .... A

3 The water body that separates Australia from an island to its south.

.... A .... S S .... R .... T

4 The capital of Australia and its only major city not located on the coast.

.... A N .... E R R ....

5 An animal native to Australia, it carries its baby in a pouch on its body.

.... A N G .... R ....

6 The world's largest structure built by living things, it can be seen from outer space.

.... R E .... T .... A R R .... R R .... F

7 The largest city of Australia, it is located on the east coast near the capital city.

.... Y D .... E ....

8 A large water body in northwest Australia.

.... NDI .... CE .... N

9 An arrangement of stars on the flag of Australia which resembles a constellation.

.... O U T .... E .... N C .... S S

10 A city famous for the largest cricket ground in Australia.

.... E L .... O U ....

Whiz Fact

The name Australia literally means 'Southern Land'. Its first official name was New Holland which was given by the Dutch.

30 Space Odyssey

Read the descriptions and write the names of some space events and celestial objects using words from the help box.

1 A space event when the moon passes between the Earth and the Sun so that we cannot see all or part of the Sun for a time. ....

2 A piece of rock from outer space that makes a bright streak across the night sky as it burns up while falling through the Earth's atmosphere. ....

3 The star that is above the North Pole in the sky. It is the brightest star in the Ursa Major constellation.

....

4 A cloud of gas and dust in outer space that can be seen in the night sky either as an indistinct bright patch or a dark outline against a brighter background.

....

5 The phase of moon during which it appears more than half but less than fully illuminated.

....

Whiz Quiz What is the special building with a curved ceiling where we can see the stars and many other celestial bodies called?

....

6 A group of stars that form a pattern in the sky. ....

7 The galaxy to which our solar system belongs. ....

8 A rocky celestial object orbiting the Sun, though its size and orbit can vary. ....

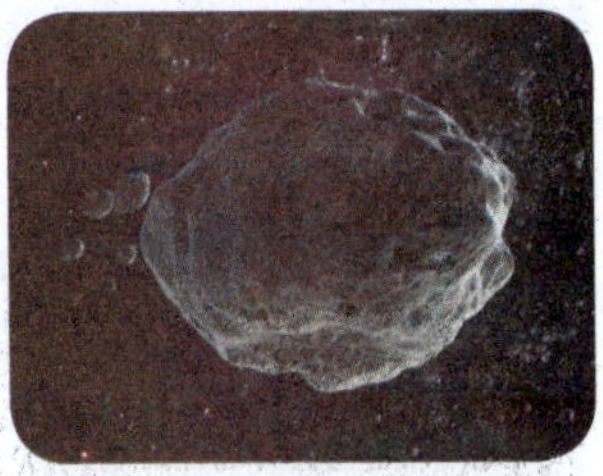

9 The Sun, the Earth, the seven planets, their moons and many other smaller celestial bodies together. ....

10 A bright celestial object with a long tail that travels around the Sun. ....

11 A dark patch or a spot that sometimes appears on the surface of the Sun. ....

Nebula Meteor Sunspot Constellation Milky Way Comet Solar eclipse North Star Solar System Gibbous Asteroid

Whiz Fact

The zodiac is an imaginary area in the sky in which the Sun, moon and planets appear to lie. The twelve signs of the zodiac have been named after constellations.

31 Presidents of India

Here is how we can remember the names of all the Presidents of India in the correct order.

1 The first President of India took over from the British Raj.

Rajendra Prasad

2 The second President was the president of all—a part of his name, *Sarv* means 'all' in Sanskrit.

Sarvepalli Radhakrishnan

3 The third President shared his surname with the tabla maestro Zakir Hussain and the artist M. F. Hussain.

Zakir Hussain

4 There are four syllables in the fourth President's name—Vi-Vi-Gi-Ri.

V.V. Giri

5 The fifth President—F for Fakhruddin and F for five.

Fakhruddin Ali Ahmed

6 The sixth President was the Speaker of the Lok Sabha before he became the president.

Neelam Sanjiva Reddy

7 The seventh President was the first Sikh president of India.

Zail Singh

8 The eighth President of India has Lord Ram's name in his name.

R. Venkataraman

9 Shankar is another name for Lord Shiva, the first name of the ninth President of India.

Shankar Dayal Sharma

10 The tenth President of India has the name of Lord Narayana in his name.

K.R. Narayanan

11 The eleventh President was renowned as the people's president and popular for his distinct hairstyle.

A.P.J. Abdul Kalam

12 The twelfth President was the first woman President of India.

Pratibha Patil

13 The initials of the thirteenth President are PM, but he was the president.

Pranab Mukherjee

Answer these questions.

1 Who was the thirteenth President of India? ....

2 Who was the second President of India? ....

3 Who was the third President of India? ....

4 V. V. Giri was President number ....

5 Zail Singh was President number ....

6 Who is the current President of India? ....

Life Skills

SAFETY

32 Safety First

A first aid kit is a box containing equipment needed to give immediate medical help in an emergency.

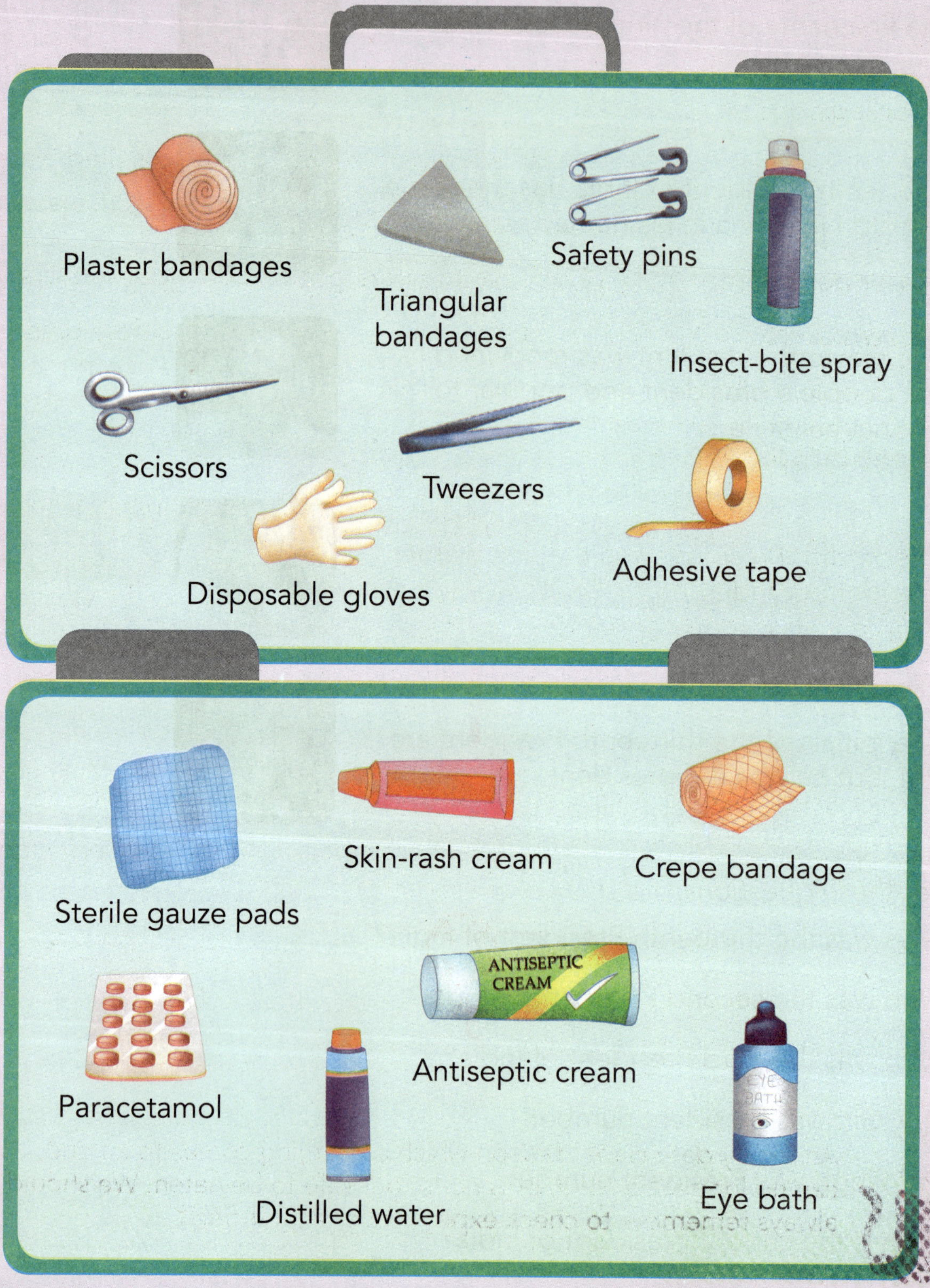

Tick (✓) the names of things from the first aid kit you will use in each of these emergency situations.

1. You sprained your ankle while running.
   - a sticking plaster
   - b crepe bandage
   - c antiseptic cream

2. You hid inside a bush while playing in the park and got red, itchy bumps on your legs.
   - a antiseptic cream
   - b skin-rash cream
   - c distilled water

3. A wooden splinter from a bench in the park got stuck in your friend's finger.
   - a tweezers
   - b scissors
   - c safety pins

4. A bee bit your ankle.
   - a antiseptic cream
   - b muscle relaxant
   - c insect-bite spray

5. A speck of dust has gotten into your eye.
   - a eye bath
   - b distilled water
   - c spectacle cleaner

6. You bruised your leg and want to clean it.
   - a painkillers
   - b distilled water
   - c antiseptic cream

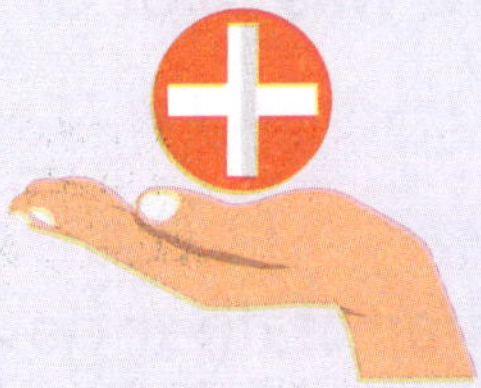

Whiz Fact

An expiry date is the date on which something comes to an end, can no longer be used, or is no longer safe to be eaten. We should always remember to check expiry dates of medicines.

33 Measuring Things

Read the paragraph and underline all the measuring words. Then write each measuring word in the correct column in the table.

Kunal was very busy on Saturday. In the morning, he went to the doctor for a checkup.

1 The doctor said he was 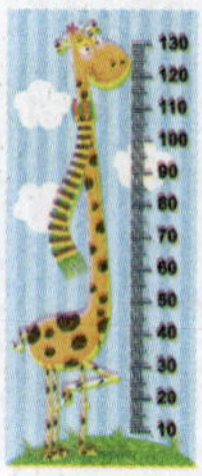 4 feet 1 inch tall and weighed 25 kilograms.

2 The nurse gave Kunal  0.5 millilitres of medicine.

3 Kunal and his father drove to the market. They bought  3 kilograms of mangoes for Kunal's grandparents.

4 Kunal's father drove  20 kilometres to reach back home. It took them  2 hours because there was a lot of traffic.

5 When they reached, Kunal's grandfather gave him a  250 millilitres box of his favourite guava juice and a  50 grams packet of potato chips.

6 Kunal's grandmother wanted him to help her measure the window because she wanted to buy new curtains. The window was  1-metre-wide.

7 They had lunch together. Kunal ate so much that when it was time for his afternoon nap, he fell asleep in  15 seconds.

Weight	
Time	
Volume	
Distance	
Length	

Whiz Quiz Write your height and weight.

....

....

Whiz Fact In the United States and some other countries, distance is measured in miles, length is measured in feet, weight is measured in pounds, and volume is measured in gallons. Most countries around the world have now adopted the metric system.

34 Grocery Shopping

Let us go grocery shopping. Look and the pictures and write C for cereals, P for pulses, O for oilseeds and S for spices.

1 

Peanuts

....

2 

Wheat

....

3 

Turmeric

....

4 

Green gram

....

5 

Oats

....

6 

Cardamom

....

7 

Mustard

....

8 

Jowar

....

9 

Kidney beans

....

Whiz Fact

The Spice Route was an ancient trade route followed by merchants, importers and exporters trading in exotic spices such as cloves and cinnamon.

35 Biodegradable Things

Biodegradable things break down or decay naturally, and can be thrown away without causing pollution. Non-biodegradable things cause pollution as they do not decompose.

Tick (✓) the biodegradable things and cross out (✗) the non-biodegradable ones.

1 

Cotton clothes

2 

Metal cans

3 

Newspaper

4 

Plastic shopping bags

5 

Rubber tyre

6 

Wood

7 

Dry leaves

8 

CDs

9 

Feathers

10 

Kitchen waste

11 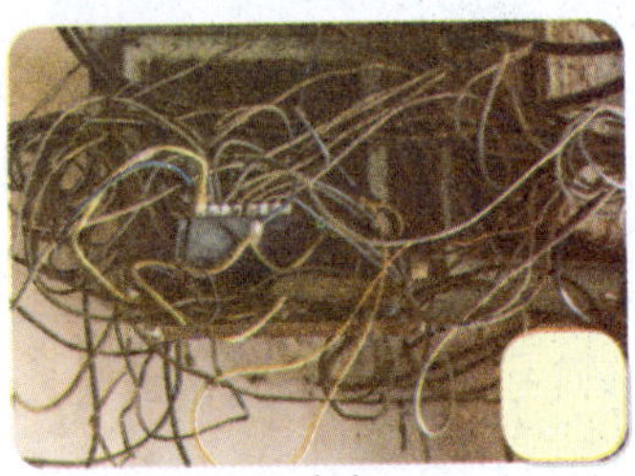

Cables

12 

Styrofoam

Whiz Fact

Plastic dumped into the sea is harmful for the sea creatures. Fish consume this plastic and die as they cannot digest it.

36 State Capitals of India

Match these Indian states with their capitals with the help of the clues.

States	Clues	Capital Cities
1 Andhra Pradesh	The proposed capital	a Bengaluru
2 Arunachal Pradesh	The name of this city means 'brick and city'	b Shimla
3 Assam	A neighbourhood in Guwahati	c Ranchi
4 Bihar	The ancient city of Pataliputra	d Chandigarh
5 Chhattisgarh	The new version of an old city	e Thiruvananthapuram
6 Goa	Located on the banks of the river Mandovi	f Bhopal
7 Gujarat	Named after the Father of the Indian Nation	g Patna
8 Haryana	Capital of two states and a union territory	h Itanagar
9 Himachal Pradesh	The Queen of Hills	i Gandhinagar
10 Jharkhand	Named after the Oraon word for bamboo grove	j Dispur
11 Karnataka	The IT capital of India	k Amaravati
12 Kerala	The southernmost state capital on the Malabar Coast	l Nava Raipur
13 Madhya Pradesh	The 'City of Lakes'	m Panaji

States	Clues	Capital Cities
14 Maharashtra	The financial capital of India	n Dehradun
15 Manipur	The Kangla Place is located here	o Agartala
16 Meghalaya	A beautiful city surrounded by the Khasi and the Garo hills	p Bhubaneswar
17 Mizoram	The only capital city with the letter 'z' in its name	q Hyderabad
18 Nagaland	The name of this city means 'the land of the kewhi flower'	r Chennai
19 Odisha	This city replaced Cuttack as the capital in 1948	s Shillong
20 Punjab	Also the capital city of Haryana	t Kolkata
21 Rajasthan	The Pink City	u Lucknow
22 Sikkim	The name of this city means 'hill top'	v Chandigarh
23 Tamil Nadu	Formerly known as Madras	w Kohima
24 Telangana	Charminar is located in this city	x Aizawl
25 Tripura	Named after Agarwood trees	y Imphal
26 Uttar Pradesh	The ancient princely state of Awadh	z Jaipur
27 Uttarakhand	Combination of two words: *dera* and *dun*	aa Mumbai
28 West Bengal	The capital of India until 1911, formerly known as Calcutta	bb Gangtok

37 Brain Teasers

Here are twelve brain teasers. Try to solve five in two minutes. Then, try to solve the other seven. Your time starts now!

1 In a single-storey orange house, everything was orange—an orange person, an orange cat, an orange fish, an orange computer, an orange chair, an orange table, an orange telephone and an orange shower. What colour were the stairs?

....

2 Arti's mother had three children. The first one was Pratham and the second one was Dwitiya. What was the name of the third child?

....

3 Two ducks in front of a duck, two ducks behind a duck. One duck each in front and behind a duck. How many ducks in total?

....

4 Which weighs more—a kilo of bricks or a kilo of feathers?

....

5 How many months have 28 days?

....

Whiz Quiz

Make two brain teasers on your own.

....

....

....

6 You are running a race. You run past the person at the second position. At what position are you running now?

7 If you keep one candy in a magic box, it turns into two candies in one minute. In another one minute, two candies double to four candies. If the magic box is full of candy in fifteen minutes, how much candy did it have at the end of fourteen minutes?

8 There are eight apples, and you take away two. How many apples will you have?

9 Imagine you are in a room filling with water. There are no windows or doors. How do you get out?

10 You are in a room at night and it is absolutely dark. You have one matchstick. Which one of these would you light first—the newspaper, the lamp, the candle, or the fire?

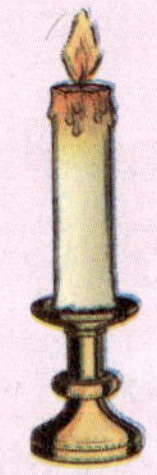

11 What appears once in a minute, twice in a moment, but never in a thousand years?

12 What travels faster: heat or cold?

38 The Wondrous Enid Blyton

Enid Blyton started writing nearly a hundred years ago, but her books have enchanted children and adults all over the world.

Match the lists of characters of some of Blyton's most popular series. Then say which series they feature in using names from the help box. One has been done for you.

Characters	Missing Characters	Names of Series
1 Julian, Dick, George, Anne	a Bumpy Dog and others	*The Famous Five*
2 Peter, Janet, Jack, Pam, Barbara	b Alison O'Sullivan, Janet Robins, Lucy Oriell and others	....
3 Pip, Bets, Larry, Daisy	c Felicity Rivers, Irene, Belinda and others	....
4 Jack, Philip, Dinah	d Silky, Moon-face, The Saucepan Man	....
5 Jo, Fanny, Bessie	e Lucy-Ann and Kiki the parrot	....
6 Darrell Rivers, Sally Hope, Alicia Johns	f Fatty and Buster	....
7 Noddy, Big-Ears, Mr. Plod	g Timmy the dog	....
8 Patricia and Isabel O'Sullivan, Hilary Wentworth, Carlotta Brown	h George, Colin, and Scamper the dog	....

The Faraway Tree *Noddy* *The Famous Five* *St. Clare's*
The Secret Seven *The Malory Towers* *The Adventure Series*
Five Find-Outers and Dog

39 Common Abbreviations

While writing, we use many short forms to save time and effort. These are called abbreviations. Several abbreviations are used in formal correspondence.

Read this letter and write the full forms of the underlined abbreviations.

Dr. Rishabh Bhatia
49A, Govind Street
Agra U.P. 223007

Date: 14 November 2019

Subject: Parcel Containing Medical Equipment

Respected Sir,

With reference to your bill no. 52682, a parcel from Arizona, United States of America weighing 4.5 kgs in a box measuring 30 x 34 x 6 cm has been dispatched at 15:00 hrs and should reach you by 16 November 2019 before 18:00 hrs. The equipment contained is worth $95 (approx. ₹6460; @ ₹68 = 1$), for which payment needs to be made.

Please pay using your credit card or e-wallet. You will receive an OTP by SMS for payment.

FYI, the box also contains a User Manual and a Warranty Card.

Regards,
For Medical Equipment Association

1 ....

2 ....

3 ....

4 ....

5 ....

6 ....

7 ....

8 ....

9 ....

10 ....

Whiz Fact

Many abbreviations in English are from foreign languages. PS stands for *post scriptum*, which is Latin for 'afterthought'. RSVP stands for *répondez s'il vous plaît*, which is French for 'please reply'.

40 Gateway of India

Read these lines about the most visited tourist attraction of Mumbai. Using the words given in the help box complete the story of the Gateway of India.

The Gateway of India is a monument located by the Arabian Sea at the southern tip of Mumbai, right opposite the iconic 1 .... It was built to commemorate the 1911 visit of 2 .... and 3 .... to Bombay, as the city was called then.

The Gateway was designed in Indo-Saracenic or Indo-Mughal style by the Scottish architect 4 .... It was built using yellow basalt and concrete and the construction was completed in 1924.

The Gateway is located on a pier called 5 .... , overlooking the Mumbai harbour. Boats from this pier ferry passengers to the 6 .... , famous for its cave temples.

In 1948, the last British soldiers marched out through the Gateway marking the end of the British Rule in India. The British who arrived by sea, ultimately left by sea and the Gateway of India became their port of departure.

Elephanta Island	Taj Mahal Palace	George Wittet
Apollo Bunder	Queen Mary	King George V

Whiz Quiz

There are two statues situated near the Gateway of India. Look at the pictures and write whose statues they are.

1 ....

2 ....

41 Sporting Terms

Write the names of the sports with which these terms are associated.

1. backstroke butterfly freestyle lap

   ....

2. dismount vault balance beam floor exercise

   ....

3. shaft arrowhead arm guard target point

   ....

4. mat pin clamp hold

   ....

5. striker dribble drive flick

   ....

6. rough green fairway par

   ....

7. deuce love-all ace twenty-love

   ....

Whiz Fact

Birdie, eagle and albatross are scores in golf. In the United States, the albatross is also called a double eagle.

42 Which Book is That?

Read the clues and select the correct words to complete the names of these books. Match the authors to the books by writing the correct letters in the boxes.

1 Every night, Charlie listens to Grandpa Joe tell stories about Mr. Willy Wonka. ☐

Charlie and the .... *Soap/Chocolate Factory*

2 Jerusha Abbott was brought up at an old-fashioned orphanage. The children were wholly dependent on charity. ☐

Daddy-Long .... *-Legs/Hair*

3 Two young children, Sally and Sam are having a very dull day. Their mother is out, and then the Cat comes in. ☐

The Cat in the .... *Hat/Hut*

4 Laura and her family live in a log cabin in the woods of Wisconsin. ☐

Little/Big .... *House on the Prairie*

5 Young Binya falls in love with a gorgeous umbrella owned by a Japanese tourist. ☐

The .... *Pink/Blue Umbrella*

6 Young Max is naughty and mischievous and not afraid of anything. ☐

Where the .... *Wild/Beautiful Things Are*

7 Ramona Quimby is no longer seven, but not quite eight, not allowed to stay home alone, yet old enough to watch pesky Willa Jean.

Ramona and her .... *Mother/Teacher*

8 Mischievous Fudge repeatedly gets into trouble. He refuses to eat for four days and swallows his brother Peter's pet turtle.

Tales of A Fourth Grade .... *Something/Nothing*

9 Matthew Cuthbert and Marilla Cuthbert are siblings who live on their ancestral farm in the quiet town of Avonlea in Prince Edward Island, Canada.

Anne/Jane .... *of Green Gables*

10 One day Lucy finds a wardrobe that transports her to a magical world.

The .... *Tiger/Lion, The* .... *Ghost/Witch, and The Wardrobe*

a 

Beverly Cleary

b 

Dr. Seuss

c 

C. S. Lewis

d 

Lucy Maud Montgomery

e 

Roald Dahl

f 

Judy Blume

g 

Laura Ingals Wilder

h 

Jean Webster

i 

Ruskin Bond

j 

Maurice Sendak

Whiz Fact

Christopher Robin was the name of A.A. Milne's son. The stories he wrote were inspired by his son's stuffed animals, especially his teddy bear.

43 Param Vir Chakra

The Param Vir Chakra is awarded for most conspicuous bravery or some daring or pre-eminent act of valour or self-sacrifice, in the presence of the enemy, whether on land, at sea, or in the air. Officers of all ranks from the Navy, the Military and the Air Force are eligible for this gallantry award.

Look at the images of the Param Vir Chakra medal and choose the correct answers.

Front

Back

1. The Param Vir Chakra medal is made of bronze/silver.
2. The medal has the flag/emblem of India in the centre.
3. The medal has four replicas of Indra's Vajra/Vishnu's Sudarshan on the front.
4. The back of the medal has the words Param Vir Chakra written in Sanskrit and Tamil/Hindi and English.
5. The flower on the back of the medal is a lotus/rose.
6. The medal is suspended from a black/purple ribbon.

Whiz Fact

The Param Vir Chakra is conferred by the President of India. A record of persons who have been awarded the Param Vir Chakra is kept in a public journal called *The Gazette of India*.

44 Equipped to Play

Every sport needs special equipment.

Find the names of sports equipment hidden in this word grid and write their names.

I	T	Y	L	E	F	G	C	S	F	C
R	B	O	A	R	D	H	L	P	R	L
O	S	T	A	R	M	H	U	E	I	U
S	U	R	F	B	O	A	R	D	N	B
C	L	E	A	T	S	D	D	L	G	E
L	G	F	O	R	E	I	G	N	D	Y
A	L	D	B	A	R	B	E	L	L	S
M	O	R	P	L	A	S	T	I	C	K
P	V	O	B	G	B	E	W	C	H	A
I	E	N	E	R	A	C	Q	U	E	T
S	S	E	N	F	T	C	O	E	Z	E
R	A	G	J	O	W	F	R	T	A	S

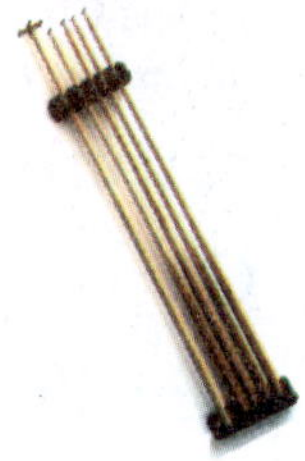

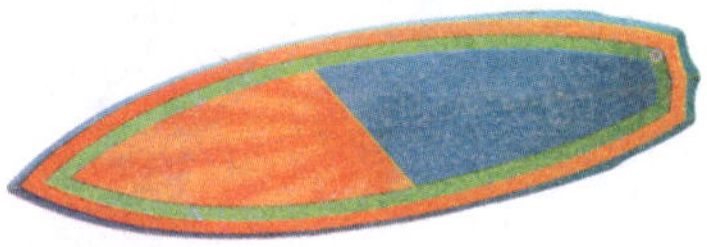

1. Squash ....
2. Golf ....
3. Baseball ....
4. Weightlifting ....
5. Boxing ....
6. Surfing ....
7. Ice skating ....
8. Snooker ....

Whiz Fact

In the book *Alice's Adventures in Wonderland*, the Queen invites Alice to play a very strange game of croquet. The equipment used are live hedgehogs, mallets and flamingos.

45 Getting Things Done

We should plan our work-time and study-time wisely to have time for fun and recreation. We can complete a task efficiently by breaking it into small steps.

Here is a project assigned to you. Arrange these pictures in the correct order so that you can complete your project in time.

Project

Prepare a short report on geography, wildlife, people and culture of any one state of India. Draw or paste pictures to show and explain things you have written about. You can base your research on the following points.

Geography: Mountains, rivers, seas, lands

Wildlife: Birds and animals found in any one state

People and culture: Languages, festivals, food habits, and clothing of the people

1

Write the report and paste pictures.

2

Print pictures found on the Internet.

3

Make a cover page for the report.

4

Buy paper, glue and any other materials needed.

5

Make a to-do list of tasks.

6

Find information on the Internet and in books.

7

Make a list of pictures needed.

8

Make timelines for each task in the to-do list.

Whiz Quiz

Which of these actions will you do to plan your daily routine?

a Make a schedule b Over-think c Do things randomly

Whiz Fact

Huge tasks such as building dams, bridges and metro lines, take years to complete. A large number of people and materials are needed to make such projects successful. The ways in which these tasks can be done is called project management.

46 Percussion Instruments

Percussion instruments make a sound when they are struck, shaken or scraped. They usually add rhythm or beat to music.

Read the clues and write the names of some percussion instruments of India using picture clues.

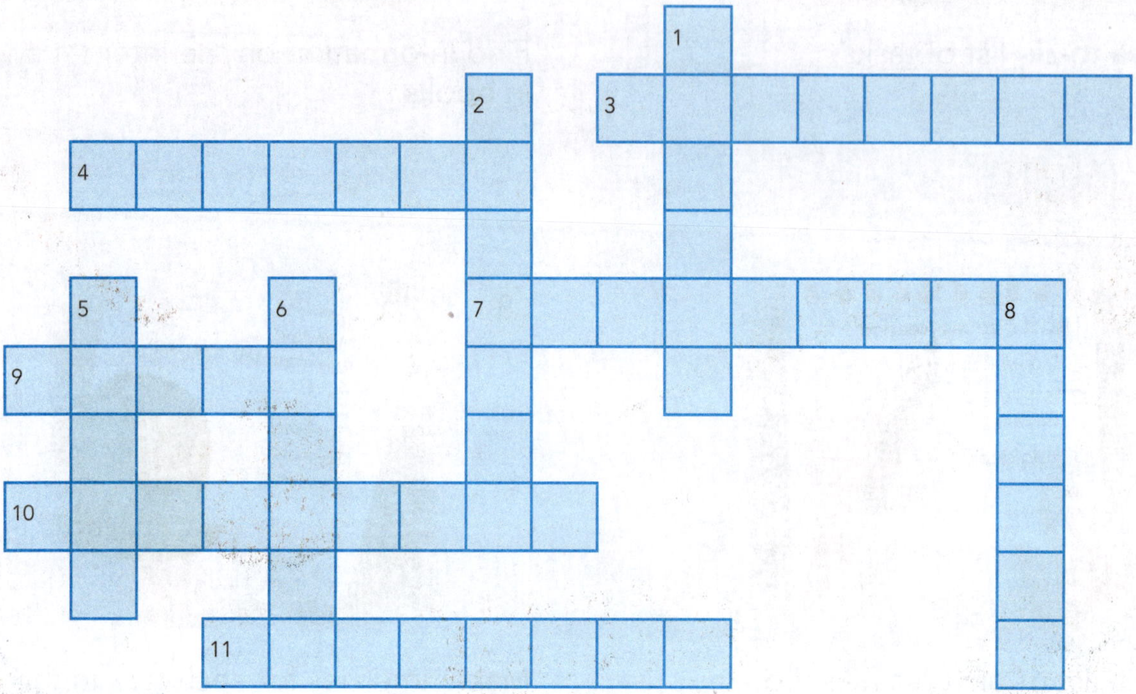

Across

3 Small metallic bells strung together, often worn as anklets

4 A folk and bhajan South Indian frame drum of the tambourine family

7 Ceramic or metal bowls tuned with water and played by striking the edges with beaters

9 Two single-headed, barrel-shaped small drums with a playing technique involving extensive use of the fingers and palms

10 Wooden double-headed drum from South India believed to have been split into two to create a popular north Indian percussion instrument

11 A barrel-shaped, two-headed drum with a low, mellow tone; it is tuned with the help of wooden wedges and ropes

Down

1 A pair of tongs with small brass jingles or rings

2 A pair of small hand-clash cymbals

5 A small two-headed drum known as the instrument of Lord Shiva

6 A bowl-shaped drum, typically played with a pair of sticks during traditional ceremonies

8 A clay pot with a narrow mouth

Mridangam

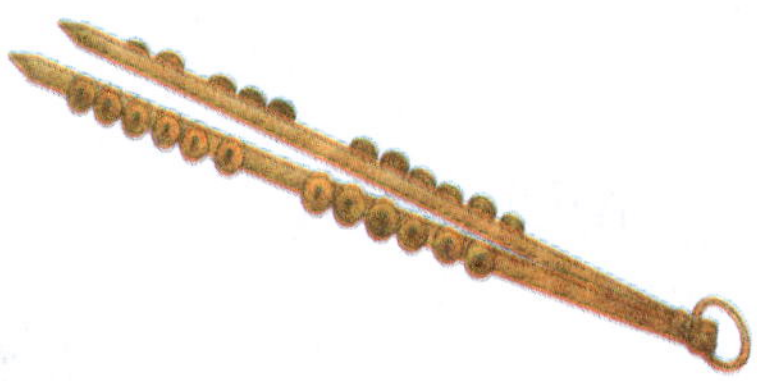

Chimta

Jal tarang

Kanjira

Ghatam

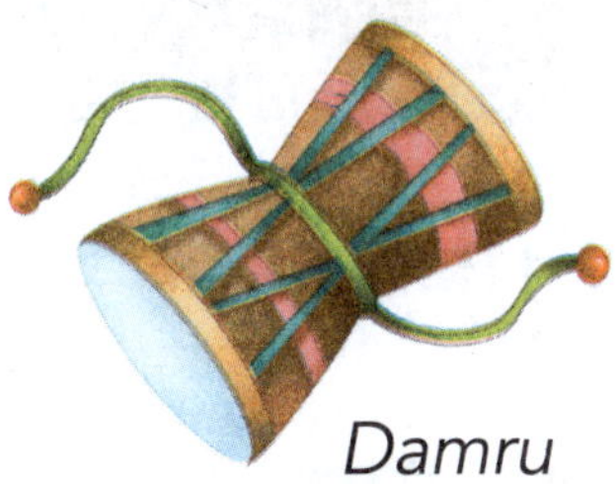

Damru

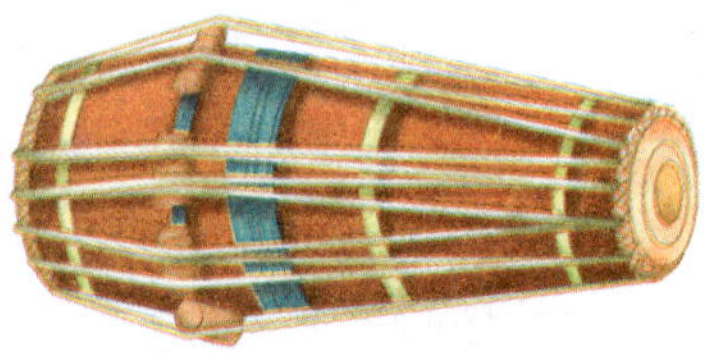

Pakhavaj

Ghungroo

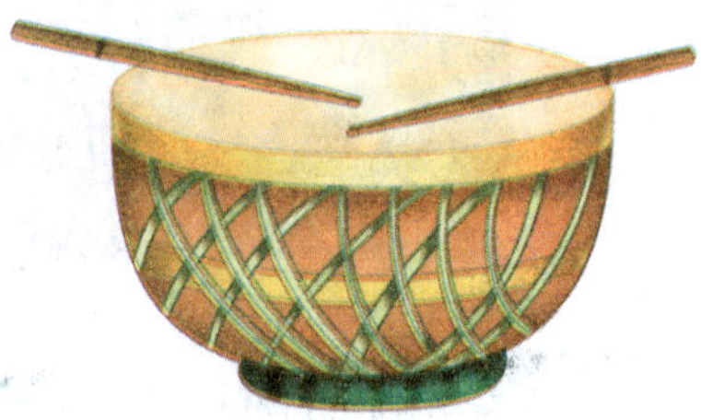

Nagara

Tabla

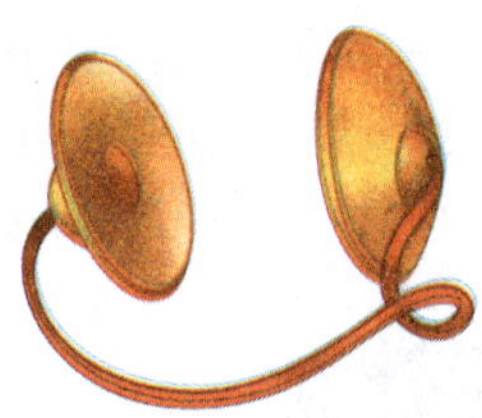

Manjira

Whiz Fact

The dholak is a two-headed hand-drum. It is a folk instrument that does not have exact tuning. It is related to the bigger dhol and the smaller dholki.

17 Wildlife of Northeast India

Northeast India has many species of birds and animals that are not found elsewhere in India.

Fill in the blanks with the correct answers.

1. The .... snow leopard/clouded leopard is the state animal of Meghalaya.

2. The Hoolock .... gibbon/gorilla is the state animal of Mizoram.

3. The gaur or .... Indian/Malaysian bison is the state animal of Nagaland.

4. The .... Purple Panda/Red Panda is the state animal of Sikkim.

5. The Phayre's langur or leaf .... monkey/bear is the state animal of Tripura.

6. The .... gayal/crocodile is the state animal of Arunachal Pradesh.

7. The one-horned .... buffalo/rhino is the state animal of Assam.

8 The Sangai or brow-antlered .... boar/deer is the state animal of Manipur.

9 Mizoram and Manipur share the same state bird, the male Mrs. Hume's pheasant. It has a long blue and .... yellow/black and brown tail.

10 The white-winged wood duck is the state bird of Assam and has black patterns on its .... white/orange head and neck.

11 The state bird of Arunachal Pradesh, the great hornbill, is notable for its black and yellow .... helmet-like/wing-like projection over its large bill.

12 The hill myna with its glossy green-black plumage and bright .... yellow-orange/ blue-green patches is the state bird of Meghalaya.

13 The state bird of Nagaland is Blyth's tragopan, a vulnerable species of pheasant with a grey belly and a .... rusty red/bottle green head.

14 The blood pheasant is the state bird of Sikkim. It has .... white/dark grey feathers.

48 Word Relationships

Let us look at some word relationships. The words to the left of the proportion sign (: :) are related in the same way as the words to the right of it. Such relationships are called analogies.

Choose the correct words to make correct word relationships.

1. FINGER : HAND : : .... : FOOT
   a Ankle   b Toes   c Toe   d Heel
2. YAWN : .... : : SMILE : HAPPINESS
   a Sleep   b Teeth   c Sadness   d Tiredness
3. .... : BOTTOM : : UP : DOWN
   a Below   b Top   c Above   d Upstairs
4. ANKLET : ANKLE : : BRACELET : ....
   a Arm   b Elbow   c Brace   d Wrist
5. DAY : WEEK : : .... : YEAR
   a Hour   b Second   c Month   d Century
6. WOMAN : .... : : GIRL : BOY
   a Man   b Person   c Husband   d Brother
7. CHATTER : MONKEY : : CLUCK : ....
   a Horse   b Hen   c Hippopotamus   d Hamster
8. .... : PLAY : : BED : SLEEP
   a Park   b Chess   c Player   d Football

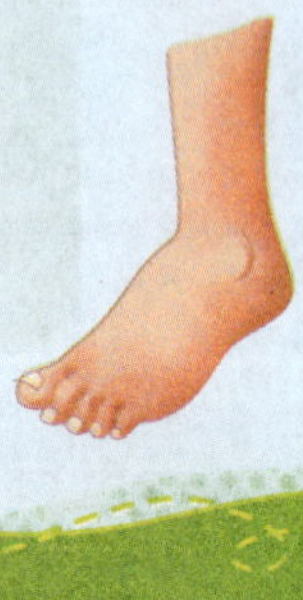

March						
				1	2	3
4	5	6	7	8	9	10
11	12	13	14	15	16	17
18	19	20	21	22	23	24
25	26	27	28	29	30	31

Quiz Yourself 1

Fill in the blanks with the correct answers.

1 The state animal of Assam is ....

2 .... is a pair of tongs with small brass jingles or rings.

3 Clubs are used in the sport of ....

4 .... is a valley in Ladakh popular for trekking.

5 .... shaped signs are used as warning road signs.

6 A .... is a word that reads the same forwards and backwards.

7 A male goose is called a ....

8 The twelfth president of India was ....

9 Green gram is a ....

10 Penguins move using their ....

11 .... is Japan's biggest island.

12 A .... is a hot spring in Himachal Pradesh.

13 A .... is a medium-sized songbird.

14 Bruises should be cleaned with ....

15 .... is the largest member of the cat family.

16 Madagascar is an .... nation.

Quiz Yourself 2

Fill in the blanks with the correct answers.

1. Kolkata is situated on the river ....
2. .... is a water body that separates Australia from Tasmania.
3. Dry leaves are .... , they decompose in nature.
4. A................................... is a group of stars called that form a pattern in the sky.
5. .... is a high-ranking official in the former imperial Chinese civil service.
6. The Param Vir Chakra medal is made of ....
7. .... is an extinct animal that was half-zebra and half-horse.
8. .... was written by Laura Ingalls Wilder.
9. .... is the backbone of a book.
10. .... is the oldest mountain range in the world.
11. The Black Diamond Express runs from .... to ....
12. .... gave the slogan *Satyameva Jayate*.
13. .... is birthday of Prophet Muhammad.
14. Dribble is a term associated with ....
15. .... is a festival celebrating the birth of the founder of the Parsi religion, Zoroaster.
16. .... wrote the book *Ramona and Her Mother*.

Answer Key

Page 9: 1. mom; 2. noon; 3. rotor; 4. kayak; 5. level; 6. wow

Page 10-11: 1. kite; 2. pelican; 3. crane; 4. bulbul; 5. frogmouth; 6. darter; 7. condor; 8. emu

Page 12: Across: 4. syringe; 5. thermometer; 7. injection; 8. antiseptic

Down: 1. bandage; 2. chemist; 3. stethoscope; 6. pill

Page 13: 1. Pink City; 2. Blue City; 3. Blue Mountains; 4. yellow; 5. Black Diamond Express; 6. Red Fort

Page 14: 1. fish; 2. penguin; 3. sea turtle; 4. frog; 5. octopus; 6. jellyfish; 7. snake; 8. stingray

Page 15: 1. jenny; 2. boar; 3. hen, rooster; 4. cow; 5. buck; 6. vixen, dog; 7. goose, gander; 8. billy; 9. stallion; 10. ewe, ram; 11. pen; 12. queen

Page 16-17: Across: 2. cheetah; 4. jaguar; 6. snow leopard; 8. leopard

Down: 1. puma; 2. clouded leopard; 3. tiger; 5. lion; 7. lynx

Page 18-19: 1. c, ii; 2. d, iii; 3. a, iv; 4. b, i; 5. h, vii; 6. g, v; 7. f, viii; 8. e, vi

Page 20-21: 1. Notes: ₹200, ₹20 Coins: 0; 2. Notes: ₹500, 50, 20 Coins: ₹2; 3. Notes: ₹500, ₹100, ₹200 Coins: 0; 4. Notes: ₹2000, ₹500 Coins: 0; 5. Notes: ₹20 Coins: ₹2; 6. Notes: ₹2000, ₹100, 10 Coins: 0

Page 22-23: 1. Fortune Cookie; 2. Dragon; 3. Compass; 4. Cheongsam; 5. Tea; 6. Hot-Air Balloon; 7. Chopsticks; 8. Lantern Festival; 9. Chinese Phoenix; 10. Great Wall of China; 11. Mandarin; 12. Lotus

Page 24-25: 1. Bhai dooj; 2. Vishu; 3. Eid ul-Fitr; 4. Khordad Sal; 5. Rath Yatra; 6. Janamashtami; 7. Gurpurab; 8. Ugadi; 9. Mahavir Jayanti; 10. Milad-un-Nabi; 11. Christmas; 12. Lohri; 13. Herath

Page 26-27: 1. planets; 2. Great Lakes; 3. Roman numerals; 4. Central America; 5. Canada; 6. European; 7. Adriatic Sea;

Page 28-29: 1. d; 2. a; 3. e; 4. c; 5. b; 6. j; 7. i; 8. f; 9. h; 10. g

Page 30-31: 1. no left turn; 2. airport ahead; 3. speed breaker ahead; 4. animal crossing; 5. no U-turn; 6. Parking; 7. narrow road ahead; 8. pedestrian crossing prohibited; 9. zebra crossing

Page 32-33: 1. *Hind*; 2. *Jayate*; 3. *Zindabad*; 4. *Mataram*; 5. *Kisaan*

Page 34: 1. f, ✓; 2. e, ×; 3. d. ✓; 4. c, ×; 5. b, ×; 6. a, ×

Page 35: 1. Bengali, Rabindranath Tagore; 2. 52; 3. Muhammad Iqbal, Urdu; 4. Ravi Shankar, *Taranah-e-Hindi*; 5. Bankim Chandra Chattopadhyay, *Anandamath*; 6. 1937

Page 36-37: 1. c; 2. e; 3. b; 4. f; 5. d; 6. a; 7. h; 8. j; 9. k; 10. m; 11. l; 12. g; 13. i

Page 38-39: 1. *Charlotte's Web*; 2. *Madeline*; 3. *Peter Pan; 4. Diary of a Wimpy Kid*; 5. *The Wizard of Oz*; 6. *Matilda*; 7. *Cat in the Hat*; 8. *Harry Potter and the Philosopher's Stone*; 9. *The Lightening Thief*; 10. *The Jungle Book*

Page 40-41: 1. Punjab; 2. Himachal Pradesh; 3. Uttarakhand; 4. Uttar Pradesh; 5. Uttar Pradesh; 6. Jammu and Kashmir; 7. Himachal Pradesh; 8. Himachal Pradesh; 9. Ladakh; 10. Punjab

Page 42: 1. Borneo, Sumatra; 2. Honshu; 3. Jamaica; 4. Madagascar; 5. Ireland; 6. Sri Lanka; 7. Cyprus; 8. Taiwan

Page 43: 1. Facebook; 2. WhatsApp; 3. Google Chrome; 4. Twitter; 5. Google Maps; 6. YouTube

Page 44-45: 1. Quagga; 2. Moa; 3. Sabre-toothed cat; 4. Mexican Grizzly Bear; 5. Passenger Pigeon; 6. Steller's Sea-Cow; 7. Javan Tiger; 8. Great Auk; 9. Dodo; 10. Woolly Mammoth; 11. Irish Elk; 12. Japanese Honshu Wolf

Page 46-47: 1. Himalayas; 2. Western Ghats, Eastern Ghats; 3. Vindhya Range; 4. Garo Hills and Khasi Hills; 5. Aravalli Range

Page 48: Across: 3. glossary; 5. index; 6. preface

Down: 1. chapter; 2. flyleaf; 4. spine

Page 49: 1. f; 2. h; 3. g; 4. e; 5. a; 6. b; 7. c; 8. d

Page 50-51: a. 9; b. 4; c. 5; d. 2; e. 6; f. 8; g. 1; h. 7; i. 10; j. 3

Page 52-53: 1. e; 2. d; 3. a; 4. b; 5. c; 6. h; 7. k; 8. j; 9. g; 10. f; 11. i

Page 54-55: 1. Perth; 2. Tasmania; 3. Bass Strait; 4. Canberra; 5. Kangaroo; 6. Great Barrier Reef; 7. Sydney; 8. Indian Ocean; 9. Southern Cross; 10. Melbourne

Page 56-57: 1. Solar eclipse; 2. Meteor; 3. Pole Star; 4. Nebula; 5. Gibbous; 6. Constellation; 7. Milky Way; 8. Asteroid; 9. Solar System; 10. Comet; 11. Sunspot

Page 58-59: 1. Pranab Mukherjee; 2. Sarvepalli Radhakrishnan; 3. Zakir Hussain; 4. four; 5. seven; 6. Ramnath Kovind

Page 60-61: 1. b; 2. b; 3. a; 4. c; 5. a; 6. b

Page 62-63: Weight: kilograms, kilograms, grams; Time: hours, seconds; Volume: millilitres; Distance: Kilometres; Length: feet, inch, metre

Page 64: 1. O; 2. C; 3. S; 4. P; 5. C; 6. S; 7. O; 8. C; 9. P

Page 65: 1. ✓; 2. ×; 3. ✓; 4. ×; 5. ×; 6. ✓; 7. ✓; 8. ×; 9. ×; 10. ✓; 11. ×; 12. ×

Page 66-67: 1. k; 2. h; 3. j; 4. g; 5. l; 6. m; 7. i; 8. d; 9. b; 10. c; 11. a; 12. e; 13. f; 14. aa; 15. y; 16. s; 17. x; 18. w; 19. p; 20. v; 21. z; 22. bb; 23. r; 24. q; 25. o; 26. u; 27. n; 28. t

Page 68-69: 1. There are no stairs in a single-storey house; 2. Arti; 3. three; 4. a kilo of bricks; 5. 12; 6. first; 7. 28; 8. 2; 9. You cannot get in if there are no doors and windows; 10. fire; 11. the letter M; 12. heat travels faster, you can catch cold

Page 70: 2. h, *The Secret Seven*; 3. f, *Five Find-Outers and Dog*; 4. e, *The Adventure Series*; 5. d, *The Faraway Tree*; 6. c, *Malory Towers*; 7. a, *Noddy*; 8. b, *St. Clare's*

Page 71: 1. doctor; 2. Uttar Pradesh; 3. number; 4. kilograms; 5. centimetres; 6. hours; 7. approximately; 8. One Time Password; 9. Short Messaging Service; 10. For Your Information

Page 72: 1. Taj Mahal Palace; 2. King George V; 3. Queen Mary; 4. George Wittet; 5. Apollo Bunder; 6. Elephanta Island

Page 73: 1. swimming; 2. gymnastics; 3. archery; 4. wrestling; 5. hockey; 6. golf; 7. tennis

Page 74-75: 1. Chocolate, e; 2. Legs, h; 3. Hat, b; 4. Little, g; 5. Blue, i; 6. Wild, j; 7. Mother, a; 8. Nothing, f; 9. Anne, d; 10. Lion, Witch, c

Page 76: 1. bronze; 2. emblem; 3. Indra's Vajra; 4. Hindi and English; 5. lotus; 6. purple

Page 77: 1. racquet; 2. club; 3. bat; 4. barbells; 5. gloves; 6. surfboard; 7. skates; 8. cue

Page 78-79: 1. 7; 2. 5; 3. 8; 4. 6; 5. 1; 6. 3; 7. 4; 8. 2

Page 80-81: Across: 3. ghungroo; 4. kanjira; 7. jal tarang; 9. tabla; 10. mridangam; 11. pakhavaj

Down: 1. chimta; 2. manjira; 5. damru; 6. nagara; 8. ghatam

Page 82-83: 1. clouded leopard; 2. gibbon; 3. Indian; 4. Red Panda; 5. monkey; 6. gayal; 7. rhino; 8. deer; 9. black and brown; 10. white; 11. helmet-like; 12. yellow-orange; 13. rusty red; 14. dark grey

Page 84: 1. Toe; 2. Sleep; 3. Top; 4. Wrist; 5. Month; 6. Man; 7. Hen; 8. Park

Page 85: 1. one-horned rhino; 2. chimta; 3. golf; 4. Zanskar; 5. Triangular; 6. palindrome; 7. gander; 8. Pratibha Patil; 9. pulses; 10. flippers; 11. Honshu; 12. Manikaran; 13. Bulbul; 14. distilled water; 15. Tiger; 16. island

Page 86: 1. Hooghly; 2. Bass Strait; 3. biodegradable; 4. constellation; 5. Mandarin; 6. bronze; 7. Quagga; 8. *Little House on the Prairie*; 9. spine; 10. Aravalli; 11. Kolkata; Dhanbad; 12. Madan Mohan Malviya; 13. Milad-un-Nabi; 14. Basketball; 15. Khordad Sal; 16. Beverly Cleary